this bread is mine

by
Robert LeFevre

Illustrations by Roy J. Hurst

AMERICAN LIBERTY PRESS

THIS BREAD IS MINE is private property.

Readers are welcome to enter and browse to their content.

It is regretted that the only way open to author or publisher to designate this book as private property is through the government copyright office. Essentially, the same chore could be performed by any good insurance firm or some other free market establishment. Since none such is in existence, and since it is deemed advisable to designate this book as private property, no choice exists for author or publisher. The book must be copyrighted, or it must be placed in that twilight realm where ownership is in doubt.

Perhaps in some future and more enlightened time authors and publishers may find a way to designate their efforts as private property without invoking the taxing powers of the government and without calling upon the police powers to hold the world at bay with the threat of violence.

Designed and printed by American Liberty Press, 161 West Wisconsin Ave., Milwaukee, Wisconsin in the United States of America.

Published in cooperation with American Liberty Press by Hydra, Inc. — a Wisconsin Corporation.

To ROSE WILDER LANE, whose book *Discovery of Freedom,*

has inspired this effort, among many, to get at the truth of

human liberty.

TABLE OF CONTENTS

PREFACE

A number of definitions of socialism are currently in vogue. Since there are various ways of defining this most important term, something other than a definition is in order. What is desirable is a framework of reference in which to set the definition. Conflicting definitions cancel out each other's usefulness. By examining the background, history and connotations of socialism it may be possible to winnow out the inconsistencies of divergent definitive terms and come at last to view socialism not so much as a single point on the landscape but as a panoramic whole. By such an approach it is hoped that a desire to grapple with socialism intellectually, rather than to react to it emotionally, will be encouraged.

There are a hundred clues all beckoning us to begin.

The word itself offers the best clue. **Social** is an adjective derived from the Latin **socius,** which means an associate or ally. The French have changed it to **socialis** and the English language has borrowed from the French.

The addition of the suffix, **ism,** has converted the adjective into a noun which connotes a distinctive doctrine, ideal, system or practice.

In combination the word **social-ism** is used to express belief in a societal system in which the essential means of production and distribution shall be collectively or governmentally owned and managed. The word conveys both an economic and a political syllogism. Socialism tends to create an ethic framework in which it is presumed that all values, rights and duties abide in the masses and that the masses must be served.

The proper antonym of socialism is individualism. Individualism presumes that individual initiative, action and interests should be independent of governmental or social control. In ethics, the conception of individualism is that all values, rights and duties originate in individuals, and not in the social whole.

Socialism and individualism are, therefore, permanently opposed doctrines.

It is the purpose of these pages to explore the relative merits of these two opposing and conflicting theories.

FOREWORD

"This Bread Is Mine" breathes the spirit of freedom. It is based upon truths of great importance. Upon them are based our individual and personal rights and freedoms. Our progress — spiritual as well as material — could not occur without those rights and freedoms.

Robert LeFevre has studied socialisms — "Christian" socialism, "scientific" socialism and other socialisms.

His treatment of "Christian" socialism — now in vogue in many churches — is the best I have seen.

"This Bread Is Mine" has excellent predecessors. In his "Wealth of Nations" (1776) Adam Smith wrote, " The property which every man has in his own labour... is the most sacred and inviolable."

LeFevre reasons rigorously from his facts and assumptions to definite conclusions. The work is almost Euclidean. The reader need not go all the way with the author to enjoy his guidance and benefit from it.

The author shows us that, in government, "there is nothing new, there is only that which has been forgotten."

— JAY MORRISON
Seattle, Washington

AUTHOR'S NOTE:

The most remarkable thing in the world is the individual human being. No possible combination of human beings is quite so unique or so fascinating as the nature and characteristics of **ONE SINGLE PERSON.**

For a number of centuries, scholars have interested themselves in the group activities of human beings. The result is an over-emphasis on groups and a corresponding under-emphasis on the importance of the single unit of the human race.

Thus, in modern times, we find an active and popular philosophy of "social-ism" with little in the way of an active and popular philosophy of individualism. It is in the hopes of making some small contribution toward such a philosophy that this book has been written.

The whole can never be greater than the sum of its parts. Society can never be more than the total of the human units which comprise it. It is from a tendency to create in the name of society a mysterious **ADDITIONAL** factor, not supplied by any of the units of society, that the doctrine of socialism takes its life.

To expound and delineate a philosophy of individualism, a beginning will be made within the doctrine of socialism, for that is the doctrine, in varying degrees, by which men have lived and to which they are fully accustomed. The errors and shortcomings of socialism will provide us an opportunity of laying the groundwork for a better understanding of ourselves as distinct and unique units. It is only when we understand our basic individual characteristics that we can journey into freedom.

Robert LeFevre
Box 165
Colorado Springs, Colorado

THIS BREAD IS MINE

CHAPTER 1

THE NAKED PREMISE

Socialism must, by definition, put society at the apex of human values. Socialism is the elevation of the mass-man to a pragmatic absolute. The leaders of socialist thought contend that all morals and all ethic values can be determined only by the results which follow a specific practice; and the results must be viewed in a societal framework.

Thus, the socialist argues that it is better to sacrifice the rights and values of an individual if by such sacrifice the masses are served — hence, the inevitable conclusion that ownership of property, especially productive property, must be on a collective basis. The thought of an individual profiting by his own efforts, while the mass-man appears not to profit, is abhorrent to all sincere socialists.

The individualist likewise serves himself with pragmatic reasoning. He concludes that any action which harms one individual must, if the process is multiplied, harm all individuals. His views of morals and ethics are essentially derived from the basis of results achieved, but with the results applied to individuals rather than to society as a whole.

No sincere individualist can condone the sacrifice of any individual's rights or values, even though in such sacrifice a majority of others may appear to benefit. The individualist takes a longer view, believing that if justice is to manifest, the sacrifice of one must be followed by a sacrifice of all. He recognizes that a single instance of sacrifice might not harm society as a whole. But he is unwilling to adopt a policy which, by the application of whim or expedient, might subsequently make him the victim of the sacrifice. Since the expedient of

"good for the whole" opens the door to "harm for the one,"
he discovers in such a policy a universal threat to his own
rights and values. In such an uncertain climate, he sees that
any individual may suddenly, and through no fault of his own,
find himself the target of "social leveling." Therefore, he concludes that the rules to govern society must be promulgated
on a base which is consistent with the best interests of each
individual in society. To hold to the contrary would effectively
eliminate all human values and rights. In fact, as the individualist reasons it, any action taken by mass man which
harms a single individual, has in large measure destroyed the
rights and values of all other individuals. He would, in fact,
prefer to run the occasional risk of one individual in society
becoming a predator against another member of society, than
support a doctrine which makes society itself a predator a-
gainst any individual in that society.

Irrespective of the isolation of a single act of injustice
perpetrated by "society" against an individual, no individualist can support it. He disdains to follow a doctrine wherein

the many can find it to their advantage to favor the sacrifice of a few. He would prefer a doctrine, similar to the Golden Rule, in which it is to the advantage of each individual to gain only through self-discipline and self-control; to acquire wealth or position by the practice of thrift and personal virtue. He insists that if a certain climate of individual human rights and values is adopted, it will be to the advantage of all to comport themselves reasonably well in this climate. On the other hand, if the uncertain climate of mass rights and mass values is substituted, then he sees there can be no fixed conditions which would encourage the practice of individual thrift and personal virtue. This is true because in dealing with society as a whole he is confronted by the baneful influences of mob psychology; by the ease with which each individual can avoid personal responsibility for his actions; by the lust and greed of some who hope to use the anonymity of mob action for their own aggrandizement.

The socialist is apt to tote up the consequences of actions in the following manner: Given an act of injustice which is harmful to 100 persons, but beneficent to 101 persons, the socialist concludes that such an act should be performed because it will bring a larger benefit (by one person) than it will bring harm.

The individualist, on the contrary, would take the position that an act of injustice which injured one person must not be performed even though a thousand others, or any number of others, might benefit thereby. The individualist would point out that a society which believed in injuring even one person for the benefit of others would be a society of cannibals. Each individual's rights are absolute.

The conflict between the two doctrines finds itself at once in an arena of morals and ethics. Let us examine, now, the socialist ethic structure, noting both its virtues and its violations.

The Socialist Ethic Premise

Here is this remarkable celestial sphere, which orbits the sun of a relatively minor solar system once every 365 and a

fraction days. This orb we call earth. It is composed of **X** a-
mounts of land area and **Y** amounts of water area. These a-
mounts may tend to shift during great global cataclysms, but
failing such tremendous natural upheavals, the ratio between
land and water remains, to all practical purposes, a constant.

It is unlikely that man, even by prodigious efforts, can
effectively alter this ratio. True, the Dutch have built dikes
and by holding back the sea have managed to regain something approximating 40 square miles of useful terrain which,
sans dikes, would be flooded by the sea at high tide. It is
possible that other peoples in future times will push back the
sea a few miles here or there. This possibility in no way dis-
turbs the fundamental premise. The basic ratio holds with
these possible deviations.

Man is a land animal. His natural habitat is found on
those surfaces of this planet which give a solid footing and
which are not forbidden him by extremes of temperature,
aridness or fluidity. Again, it could be noted that man has
managed to overcome some of his basic difficulties in dealing

with the non-land surfaces and the land surfaces which are normally hostile to him. But these minor deviations in no way destroy the fact that man's natural habitat is terra firma, and that on the land surfaces he survives best in temperate zones and at altitudes below 7,000 feet.

If we permit X to represent all the inhabitable land of earth, and if we cause A to represent all of the people who are on the earth at this time, then we have a constant — the relationship between total number of people and total amounts of land available for purposes of survival. It becomes a simple arithmetic problem to discover just how much land would be available for each person if it were to be shared pro-rata.

It is at once obvious that man's material well-being is directly related to the numbers of persons living at a given moment and the amount of suitable land available for all of them.

The equation could be shown thus: $\frac{X}{A} = MMW$. All of the land, divided equally among all of mankind, is equated with man's material well-being. Such a division will provide a moral footing for a society of equal shares.

This is socialist thinking. The purist of socialist conviction would hold that each human being should be entitled to a pro-rata share of the livable land areas; that any human being who obtained more than this precise amount would have obtained it through criminal action of one sort or another, since he could not possibly have a moral claim upon it.

Likewise, it would be held that any person who had less than his pro-rata share has, through some type of criminality, been deprived of what is rightfully his.

This highly theoretical and idealistic fallacy has long been abandoned by socialists. But it is important that it be stated, for despite its abandonment, socialist minds continue to polarize themselves to the false notion. They now admit that the attainment of such a system is totally impossible. Yet, having admitted it, they strive to come as close to the impossibility as can practically be achieved.

The reason for the abandonment is obvious. No two pieces of land are of equal value. Some land has a multiplicity of uses and as such is highly desirable for dwelling purposes, commerce, manufacture, agriculture, mining and the like. Other parcels have scarcely any use at all. And the fluctuations of usage, varying from age to age, and from clime to clime, make anything like a simple arithmetic division of land on a per capita basis not only futile but ridiculous. Thus, to arrive at a just distribution of the X in the equation is impossible.

However, the socialist has no better luck when he attempts to postulate the equality, and therefore the deservingness, of the A in the equation, man. Like the land, human beings contain in their individual natures enormous variables. Some men have numerous attributes and skills which serve to enhance their worth. Others appear to have few if any such virtues.

Alas, the socialist at this point of his thinking would have to abandon his entire premise and dismiss the whole theory as an impractical though roseate dream, were it not for the emergence of a second idea, which has been promoted skillfully and with vigor, particularly during the past several centuries.

The second idea, which is sort of a defense in depth behind the false premise of human equalness and the equally false notion of equal land division, is that what may not be equal by nature, can be made equal by legislation.

Summons to Violence

Here the socialist enjoys his most exhilarating moment. If it is true, and it is demonstrably true, that the world has been so ordered that at the beginning, land and people are unequal, then the equality can be obtained at the end, by force, rather than at the beginning by division.

This is a delightful idea to any person who wishes to intervene in the lives of others. The socialist now confines himself not to production, but to distribution. He is no longer interested in trying to obtain either land or human equality as a fixed condition, on which to base his theories. He is content with the inequalities as he finds them.

But, by the power of legislation, he will take the inequalities and from the end product work backward, hewing and hacking until everything is leveled to a desirable sameness.

Let one man produce $100,000 worth of goods and a second man only $15,000 in a corresponding period of time. What does it matter? The socialist can step in, take 90% from the first man, $33\frac{1}{3}$% from the second man, leaving both with the value of $10,000, and meanwhile he can distribute the balance to a number of persons who have produced nothing, and at the same time pay himself a fine wage for managing the distribution.

Here is the emergence of the socialist ethic. It is this. *No human being on this planet is entitled to more of the good things that this planet provides than any other human being. If one man produces more than he needs, it is of benefit to all that he be compelled to share the excess with others.* Nor can this be considered a robbery, for if we return to the first myth, we find that no man has a right to more than any other man and, consequently, if a man produces more than he himself needs, it follows that he has produced it for others and no time should be lost in getting it into the hands of others.

So here is the socialist world with a moral base which is pleasing to socialists. It has both an economic and political application. The commandments are two in number — the first, economic; the second, political: Thou shalt have no more than the least of thy fellows; and, to cause those who have more than others, to give up what they have for the benefit of others, is the highest virtue.

There is too large a tendency in non-socialist circles to greet these commandments with contempt and without grasping the socialist motivation. Whether the facts of life coincide with these beliefs is not altogether the only thing to be considered. There is a sort of goodnesss here, a longing for love and compassion, a belief that men should help each other, a sort of high-minded missionaryism which is aimed at obviating the miseries of the poverty-stricken, the lowly, the poorly paid and the humble. That this doctrine has an appeal to a large segment of the people of this planet is attested to on every hand.

We have only to observe the socialist legislation passed in the last three decades in virtually every governmentalized society in the world to recognize its wide appeal.

Christian Beginnings

We have only to peer into the Christian doctrine to find that from the time the apostles began to preach, a sort of socialist longing pervades much of the gospel teachings.

"And the multitude of them that believed were of one heart and of one soul: neither said any of them that ought of the things which he possessed was his own; but they had all things common.

"And with great power gave the apostles witness of the resurrection of the Lord Jesus: and great grace was upon them all.

"Neither was there any among them that lacked: for as many as were possessors of lands or houses sold them, and brought the prices of the things, that were sold,

"And laid them down at the apostle's feet: and distribu-tion was made unto every man according as he had need." (The Acts IV, 32-35)

This had a most persuasive effect upon the new converts.

"But a certain man named Ananias, with Sapphira his wife, sold a possession,

"And kept back part of the price, his wife also being privy to it, and brought a certain part, and laid it at the apostle's feet.

"But Peter said, Ananias, why hath Satan filled thine heart to lie to the Holy Ghost, and to keep back part of the price of the land?

"Whiles it remained, was it not thine own? and after it was sold, was it not in thine own power? thou hast not lied unto men but unto God.

"And Ananias hearing these words, fell down, and gave up the ghost; and great fear came on all of them that heard these things." (The Acts V, 1-5)

Nor did this terrible and apparently divine punishment descend upon Ananias alone, but the scriptures go on to reveal that his wife returned about three hours later, not knowing that her husband was already dead and buried. Peter accuses her of trying to retain a portion of what was hers and confronts her with her husband's death. Sapphira obligingly falls dead, too.

This double catastrophe inflicted apparently from on high, must have assisted the early fund-raising efforts enormously, and served the cause of total sharing. One can imagine the fear which swept these early socialists as they whispered among themselves the dread punishment to overtake any person who attempted to keep more of this world's goods than his fellows.

But one must look to modern times to find as bold and revolutionary an utterance as is found in the scriptures in the book of James. Chapter II, 5-6 reads: "Hearken, my beloved brethren, hath not God chosen the poor of this world rich in faith, and heirs of the kingdom which he hath promised to them that love him?

"But ye have despised the poor. Do not rich men oppress you, and draw you before the judgment seats?"

And to conclude this theme we find in Chapter V, verses 1-4, the author of the book of James saying:

"Go to now, ye rich men, weep and howl for your miseries that shall come upon you.

"Your riches are corrupted, and your garments are moth-eaten.

"Your gold and silver is cankered; and the rust of them shall be a witness against you, and shall eat your flesh as it were fire. You have heaped treasure together for the last days.

"Behold, the hire of the labourers who have reaped down your fields, which is of you kept back by fraud, crieth: and the cries of them which have reaped are entered into the ears of the Lord of sabaoth."

A modern labor leader would have to extend himself to surpass this socialist acid.

There is small wonder, in the face of such teachings, that socialism flourishes. When mankind's most beautiful and exalted religion, together with its most advanced and progressive governments, alike adopt creeds of this sort, the popularity of any kind of share-the-wealth scheme is easily predictable.

So, it is insufficient to sneer at the socialist ethic and pronounce it unnatural, unrealistic and destructive both of men's goods and men's ambitions.

True Radicals Are Individualists

who, when?

Methodist Bishop G. Bromley Oxnam, who has frequently been the target of scorn, and others active in the social gospel work have a sound footing deep within the history of the early church. We may discover, with the advantage of perspective and the penetration of research, that Oxnam and his numerous cohorts are the true conservatives of the faith and are attempting to adhere to the fundamental socialism of the first devotees of Christianity. Likewise, it may prove that the rising tide of alleged conservatism in the theology of Christendom is, in fact, the radical element which is seeking not to maintain the tradition of the early church, but to write a new one, based more upon the sound economics of the parable of the talents than upon the socialist teachings and practices of the apostles.

In modern times the schism in our churches is growing more apparent with each passing day. The radical element, led by such ecclesiastics as the Reverend Carl McIntire of Collingswood, New Jersey, the Reverend James W. Fifield, Jr., of the First Congregational Church of Los Angeles, the Reverend Howard E. Kershner of "Christian Economics," and scores of others who are at odds with socialism, has decorated the individualist position with high purpose and integrity.

There are numerous lay organizations, also, which have endeavored to emphasize sound economics and the individualist view. Among these are Spiritual Mobilization of San Jacinto, California, the American Council of Christian Laymen led by Verne P. Kaub of Madison, Wisconsin, and the Circuit Riders of the Methodists under the leadership of M. G. Lowman of Cincinnati.

Despite these radical anti-socialist efforts, by all odds the largest and most powerful (numerically) side is that of the socialist phalanx. The ecumenical movement designed to create a world church, to merge all gospel teachings into a single controlled center, and to further the social concepts of sharing wealth, has gained ground steadily. The conservatives who seek to preserve the Christian ethic as something favorable to socialism, have obtained the advantage, both of weight and finances.

On the Catholic side of the Christian front the schism is not as clearly defined. From the rise of Marxism in the 19th century, Catholics have disdained in the main to succumb to the blandishments of the share-the-wealthers. Still, the modern labor movement represents their Achilles' heel. There are a few who, including Dean Clarence Manion, have stood their ground against the collusion represented by a combine of big labor and big government with the inevitable erosion of individual freedom. But there are only a few.

From the standpoint of human liberty and individual freedom, however, the church in general is no longer a refuge.

Early Beginnings

If we consider the early history of the Christian church, it preserves its most tender and appealing record in service to the poor. Nor would it be either accurate or just to ascribe the preaching against wealth exclusively to the apostles.

Matthew, who brings us the Sermon on the Mount, has Christ begin his admonitions: "Blessed are the poor in spirit: for theirs is the Kingdom of Heaven."

Luke has our Lord extending the thought in his XIV Chapter, 12, 13 and 14 verses. "Then said he also to him that bade him, When thou makest a dinner or a supper, call not thy friends, nor thy brethren, neither thy kinsmen, nor thy rich neighbors; lest they also bid thee again, and a recompense be made thee.

"But when thou makest a feast, call the poor, the maimed, the lame, the blind:

"And thou shalt be blessed; for they cannot recompense thee: for thou shalt be recompensed at the resurrection of the just."

Economists who review our Lord's summation are confronted with the melancholy duty of concluding that a reasonable exchange between contemporaries or equals is somehow less desirable than an outright grant to the improvident and the unfortunate.

Yet, in the same instant the economist recognizes the moral certainty of any voluntary two-way exchange, and discovers an area of uncertainty, so far as morality is concerned, when any kind of something-for-nothing philosophy is invoked.

The problem becomes acute when the economic philosopher recognizes that the arrangement advocated is a something-for-nothing arrangement only insofar as the two active persons in the transaction are concerned, for an exchange is promised. If A will give to B in this world and B is unable to return the favor, A should rejoice, because C, in the next life, will reward A. What happens to B in the next life is uncertain.

But this is strange economic counselling. B apparently has a single responsibility. He must be unforunate. The lucky chance of his poverty makes A's future brighter with the prospects of reward.

What is particularly pertinent is the almost inevitable supposition in the mind of the poor or unfortunate that it is the Christian duty of others to take care of them. This supposition could lead and most certainly has led to the concept of dependency — of some persons being perpetually inferior and thus legitimately assuming the manner and function of parasites.

In the book of Mark, Chapter X, verses 23-26, we find these words:

"And Jesus looked around about, and saith unto his disciples, How hardly shall they that have riches enter into the kingdom of God!

"And the disciples were astonished at his words. But Jesus answereth again, and saith unto them, Children, how hard is it for them that trust in riches to enter into the kingdom of God!

"And they were astonished out of measure, saying among themselves, Who then can be saved?"

Christ removes their wonderment by assuring them that with God all things are possible and that, difficult though it may be, God can work the miracle and save the rich man if He so chooses.

Clearly, in the mind of the great teacher, riches provide an obstacle to heaven. Thus, when his disciples after him intone even more vigorously against wealth, it is scarcely to be wondered at.

There is, of course, the argument that Jesus was reminding his disciples that "you can't take it with you." And if this utterance can be interpreted to mean that a desire for worldly goods should not dominate the consciousness of the individual producer and entrepreneur, but rather be taken in stride, it becomes, in fact, a useful argument for the individualist who wants something more from life than the amassment of this world's goods.

But since the socialists can also employ the quotations, demonstrating that Christ believed the Lord to have an aversion to wealth to such an extent that entrance into heaven by a man of means was seriously impaired, the usefulness of the utterances in the individualist camp is seriously restricted.

Considering the nature of life and the problems which accompany successful production, whether in a freely competitive market place or otherwise, it becomes open to question if a man can attain great wealth unless he puts his mind to it, to the exclusion of other things. And since the accumulation of great wealth is a necessary adjunct to the procurement of the tools of production, which fact will be discussed more fully later, a certain singleness of purpose at the financial level is mandatory or the system of individualistic capitalism is doomed. Though wealth for its own sake is scarcely commendable, wealth as a device to further production is essential. And since by its nature, wealth that is hoarded does not increase, but wealth that is invested does, it appears that an honest desire to increase wealth is a prime essential to capitalism. Nor can such a desire be described as heinous or destructive. On the contrary, our manifold blessings in an individualistic and capitalistic economy are directly traceable to this desire.

It becomes debatable, therefore, if a desire on the part of some which leads to so much benefit to others, is automatically conducive to a detour in the route to heaven.

To its credit, the modern church has been less harsh than Peter. It has extolled the virtue of voluntary giving and as a rule has stood opposed to any forceful collecting of tithings. Essentially, the Christian ethic, if we take this ancient part of it, belongs to the economic syllogism and not to the political.

What appears almost miraculous is the transformation of the church from the days of its beginnings into something which at least in the Western world approximates a successful commercial enterprise. Though many and vigorous have been the preachments against the accumulation of wealth, both by ancient leaders and modern crusaders, the church itself has scarcely stood as an emblem of the blessed poverty it at first supported.

Renan, in his study of the great caesar, "Marc Aurele," indicates that the early Christians had followed the Essenes and agreed with that ancient Jewish sect that a prosperous man who does not share his surplus with the poor is a thief, thereby providing the foundation for Marx's later phrase, "a dollar of profit is an unpaid wage," and for Proudhon's dictum, "property is robbery."

Emergency Institution

Economically speaking, although the concept of universal sharing of all wealth may forever have its appeal, the practice is consumptive and not productive. And we can excuse our early Christian forebears for their failure to support a sound economy, for the early church was an emergency institution set up to preserve the teachings of Jesus until he came a second time.

One has only to examine the formation of the first Christian group called Ebionim in Syria, which means "the poor," to recognize that these early followers of Christ expected the end of the world and that they were simply marking time until that day should come. The expectation of the end of creation doubtless spurred the idea of communal sharing.

It is a simple matter to conclude, if one believes in the imminent destruction of all creation, that property has little value. Read Paul. He takes no stand for human liberty, for independence, for thrift and a soundly applied economic system. He warns his various **ekklesia** to prepare themselves for the second coming. Peter appears to be of like mind. And James reminds his hearers that the "coming of the Lord draweth nigh."

Under the pressures inherent in an impinging last judgment there would be little merit and less consistency in urging any kind of procedure that would tend to make man's lot on this planet a more pleasing and profitable one. It is not difficult to excuse the early Christians their drift toward socialism. What is more difficult is to excuse the present-day exponents of Christ who preach the same faulty economics.

But it should be remembered that whatever the preachments in the first few centuries after Christ, there was little effort to invoke compulsion. If you elected to surrender all your wealth to the church, as Peter urged, the choice was your own. The merit of the surrender lay in its voluntary nature.

And here is the first lesson to be learned respecting socialism. For it has both a relatively harmless application and a totally harmful one. The idea of wealth-sharing, when the sharing is voluntary, is not a fundamental violation of human rights. It may fly in the face of reality from a standpoint of sound economics. But it is scarcely an abridgment of the doctrines of individualism, so long as persuasion takes the place of compulsion.

Indeed, one can almost grow misty-eyed as he thinks of those first devotees of the new gospel, sacrificing everything they had, property, customs, even wives and children, and under duress their very lives, in the supposition that the Lord was coming for them momentarily and that whatever occurred, they would be saved.

In any case, we see here the long and honorable record of socialist economic fallacy. *The socialist persists in viewing man, not as an individual creature, but as a mass-man.* And this is true even when the mass is Christian, and the mass-man to be considered is the total Christian community. The socialist elevates society to the moral heights. It is the good of the whole that matters to him. [Any minority is always expendable if only the majority can gain by the sacrifice.]

Imagine a world in which there are no poor; in which all things are shared equally by all men according to their need. This is the dream of the socialist. We will next examine the various methods employed by socialists to bridge the gap between their dream and the realities of life.

CHAPTER 2

LOINS OF BRASS

A method or procedure implies first a logical body of thought and then some means of making it work. To begin with, socialists had neither.

It has been shown that socialist ideas were not foreign to Christianity in its infancy. And it has been noted that the idea of sharing wealth was a familiar one to the Essenes, which sect predated the birth of Christ by an estimated thousand years. We could, in fact, return to Hammurabi and discover that his first written code of law (circa 3,000 B.C.)

was aimed in part at controlling the wealthy and compelling largesse to the poor.

Socialism a Fantasy

Socialism, in all probability, is one of those persistent myth forms which crop up among nearly every people in their primitive days. It is a dream, a childish vision that imagines the world to be other than it is. The same minds that image a socialist society have dreamed of fairies, goblins, dragons and other fantasies.

The dream, so long as it remains but a dream, is harmless. Or, as the early Christians practiced it, without duress and voluntarily though it is contrary to the laws of nature, it is not too great a burden.

It remained for someone to organize the dream of socialism and to present it in logical and cogent form. The man who first and most successfully performed this task predates the Christ by some 400 years. It is doubtful if Jesus ever heard of him.

He was born in Egina of aristocratic parents about the year 427 B.C. His name was Aristocles, but because he was a fine soldier and a prize-winning athlete with broad shoulders, he was called Plato. It is to Plato we must look for the first and most profound delineation of the collectivist dream.

Of all the Greek writers, only Plato and Xenophon have been transmitted to posterity in toto. All other ancient Greeks are fragmentations. So Plato is complete and his arguments in context.

It is from Plato that we learn most of Socrates. Plato was a student at the feet of the greatest of the Sophists. At the age of 28 he attended Socrates when he drank the poisoned hemlock administered to him by democratic verdict. The injustice of the sentence inflicted upon the harmless wizard of philosophy so touched the youth that he put away his athletic proclivities and dedicated his life to the destruction of democracy. Having tasted the heady wine of Socratic debate with the master of interrogation, all other pursuits seemed to him dull by comparison. Plato became the world's foremost philosopher.

His dialogues are a treasure of amusing egg-headedness. But his "Republic," the very core of his aim and purpose in life, sums up the man. Of this work Will Durant in his "Story of Philosophy" says, "Here we shall find his metaphysics, his theology, his ethics, his psychology, his pedagogy, his politics, his theory of art. Here we shall find problems reeking with modernity and contemporary savor: communism and social-ism, feminism and birth-control and eugenics, Nietzschean problems of morality and aristocracy, Rousseauian problems of return to nature and libertarian education, Bergsonian **elan vital** and Freudian psychoanalysis — everything is here."

Emerson, in his essay on Plato, gives the warmest praise. "Plato is philosophy, and philosophy Plato." He even borrows the words of Omar in praise of the Koran and says of Plato's "Republic," "Burn the libraries, for their value is in this book."

Nor is this gush of sentiment respecting the "Republic," and its author, undeserved. Even in translation, the "Republic" sparkles with much wit and wisdom, as it craftily and subtly lays the groundwork for at least two dozen centuries of error.

Plato had seen democracy at work in Athens. He despised it. Long and valiantly he argued that it would produce the worst of societies, the cruelest and the least just of governments.

He considers the doctrine of universal suffrage as an invitation to fools to rule their betters. He reminds us that when we are ill, we seek a skilled physician, not a democratic prescription written by a mob. And he compares the illness of the person to the illness of a state. If the state is sick, he suggests, how foolish to entrust its cure to the ignorance and vainglory of the populace at large. What do they know as a collective? The problem is to select, not the most popular, the finest orator, the most unscrupulous mendicant to applause, but the most skillful ruler. How do we go about finding such a paragon? Ah. This is the burden of the "Republic."

Platonic Metals

Plato weaves a giant tapestry of political and psychological theory. He divides all of humanity into three classes — the gold, the silver and the brass. The brass are those who are motivated by desire. And desire, says the Greek sage, is seated in the loins. Men of brass are those who seek to satisfy themselves with money and with manufacture. These are the least useful personages in society, he declares, and thereby sets the stage of Shi Huang-ti in far Cathay who built the Chinese wall with conscript labor, most of which was recruited violently from the marts of trade and commerce. Men of brass are given over to their lusts and to vain display. He does not hate them. He simply wishes to relegate them to the lowest rung.

Men of silver, Plato says, are motivated not so much by lust and desire as by emotion. Their center is in the heart, their medium is blood. These men care not what they fight for, because what they want is victory. They are unburdened with scruples. They make the finest soldiers. The warrior class is far above the merchant class in Plato's book. And here he sets the stage for all recorded history thus far which in the main has been a recitation of wars and conquests, with moral certainty awarded to the strongest troops.

And then the men of gold. These are rare, says Plato, and all the more valuable because of scarcity. These are the intellects, the men of mind and genius; in short, these are the philosophers. Perhaps his love of philosophers can be forgiven. It is a strange perversion when a self-chosen field is considered less than the very best by its own chooser. What we must have is the king who is also a philosopher. Or, if you will, the philosopher must be made the king.

How can this be brought about? Plato has the answer for this question, too. Not by elections, but by education. [Children must be separated from their parents and trained by the state.] Otherwise, the follies of the elders will surround and color the impressionable minds. He gives a long and carefully delineated series of steps with periodic testings which are calculated to cause the metals each to seek its Platonic level.

The schooling and the testing occupy the first years of each individual's life. The brass is drained out first so life goes on. Though Plato doesn't give credit to his men of brass, life for the others rests on their production. The silver falls through the sieve by the age of 30. But the true philosopher undergoes additional training and testing until he reaches the ripe old age of 50. Only then is he considered fit to rule.

A government by aristocrats is what Plato wants. And this, he says, is the true republic. Alexander Hamilton thought so, too, at the founding of this nation. But though all the American founding fathers were not convinced of these philosophic claims to political ascendency, it is doubtless true that most of them were convinced, as was this great Greek, that democracy is a snare and a delusion.

We see in Plato the emergence of the socialist super-state, albeit run by gentle and kindly men of wisdom. And if we consider the Russian pattern, modeled after Marx, we marvel how much Marx borrowed from the Greek. In Russia, children are taken from their mothers at the age of six months, and the state provides the education. State education is the tenth plank in the Communist Manifesto. Even Hitler saw the wisdom of building a state by controlling young minds. And Christianity has long held that the child before the age of seven must be drilled in the necessary beliefs if he is to be secure in Christ.

But let us make no mistake about the Platonic theory. Here is the beginning of the political syllogism. Mark how it ties in to the economic line of reasoning. This, too, is Plato:

"In the first place none of them should have any property beyond what is absolutely necessary; neither should they have a private house, with bars and bolts, closed against any one who has a mind to enter; their provisions should be only such as are required by trained warriors, who are men of temperance and courage; their agreement is to receive from the citizens a fixed rate of pay, enough to meet the expenses of the year, and no more; and they will have common meals and live together, like soldiers in a camp. Gold and silver we will tell them that they have from God; the diviner metal is within them, and they have therefore no need of that earthly dross which passes under the name of gold, and ought not to pollute the divine by earthly admixture, for that commoner metal has been the course of many unholy deeds; but their own is undefiled. And they alone of all the citizens may not touch or handle silver or gold, or be under the same roof with them, or wear them, or drink from them. And this will be their salvation and the salvation of the State. But should they ever acquire homes or lands or moneys of their own, they will become housekeepers and husbandmen instead of guardians; enemies and tyrants instead of allies of the other citizens; hating and being hated, plotting and being plotted against, they will pass thru life in much greater terror of internal than of external enemies; and the hour of ruin, both to themselves and to the rest of the State, will be at hand."

Will the wives of these men of silver be content without ornamentation and the finer things of life? Plato has the answer for that, too. The guardians will have no wives, but will have a socialism in wives as well as in goods. They will share even these delicacies in common. But not indiscriminately, please. The state will supervise each amorous embrace. And all of the guardian mothers will give birth to all of the guardian children, and all are property of the state and must be trained and tested by the state to take their rightful places in society at the proper time.

Marx was to paraphrase this when he urged the abandonment of family and family ties, a matter which will be discussed in greater detail in a later chapter.

The Super State

So, this is Plato, a great mind, a flowering plant of bright crimson petals. With him, the state was everything. Individuals below the status of Ph.D.'s were so many units to be controlled and regimented. Only the philosopher was to be free, to sit in company with other philosopers and to dream even greater dreams of truth.

This is the classic pyramid structure of all government. There will be a broad base of artisans and workers who will own property privately but will be taxed to see that no excess of wealth or property accrues. There will be a narrower class of warriors sitting on top of the common herd, impecunious and paid by the state, but producing nothing. And at the top of the pyramid, a small select group of wise men who will govern and control all other men.

Here is the socialist dream put into a model that supposedly would work. All it needs is the political disregard of human rights by some bold and powerful warlord who would begin with little children.

It might be of value here to refer to a speech by Professor Arnold J. Toynbee, at the philosophical society of Edinburgh University as reported in Time Magazine, November 12, 1952. According to this magazine report, Toynbee predicted that within half a century, the planet will be united politically through concentration of irresistible military power. The American Empire of 2002, like the Roman Empire of Augustus, will make use of "constitutional fictions." . . . "democracy will have receded in the current western use of the term, as meaning self-government. It may have advanced in the current Russian usage, as meaning social equality in contrast to hierarchy of classes. The loss of freedom on the material plane will have been the price of abolition of violence and injustice on the material plane. 'Government is the penalty for original sin.' Given the imperfection of human nature, the only way to abolish strife and injustice on the material plane is to restrict freedom there. In a powerful, healthy, over-populated world, even the proletarian's freedom to beget children will no longer be his private affair, but will be regulated by the state." Plato's idea of a totally controlled and regimented population dies hard.

In sum, though Plato wrote 2,000 years ago, his carefully drawn symposium of thought has been acted upon only rarely. But the influence of this man's ideas has been enormous and persevering. Christianity itself, which began with oriental mysticism and symbolism, was in the first three centuries after Christ reworked by the Greek mind, largely influenced by the Platonic school.

Durant says, "Much of the politics of Catholicism was derived from Plato's 'royal lies' or influenced by them: the ideas of heaven, purgatory, and hell, in their medieval form, are traceable to the last book of the 'Republic' . . . even the educational 'quadrivium' (arithmetic, geometry, astronomy and music) was modeled on the curriculum outlined by Plato."

Plato, the father of philosophy, had carried forward the socialist dream. But the dreamers between the time of Plato and the time of Lenin were not content merely to dream, although they did a great deal of dreaming.

We will touch upon only two more dreams put into organized form which fall far short of filling up this gap in time. Like Plato, these more current dreamers wanted the socialist absolute. Unlike him, they were not bold enough, or clever enough to figure out a way to cross the chasm between the fantasy of universal sharing, and the grim reality of life.

CHAPTER 3

WILD SEEDS

The time is the reign of Henry VIII of England. The author is Sir Thomas More, a learned and respected member of the king's court. At the moment, he is the king's ambassador to Flanders. While there, in 1515, he was to write a visionary and fictional treatise which would go down in history as a socialist classic. Later, he would be present with King Henry at the Field of the Cloth of God. He would become speaker of the House of Commons in 1523. He would finally succeed Wolsey as chancellor of England. And then, a great cloud would cross his fair name. For he would find himself unwilling to take the oath of adherence to the act vesting the succession of the crown in the issue of Anne Boleyn. The argument between Sir Thomas and his king centered in Henry VIII's wishes to obtain a divorce from Catherine of Aragon and to marry again. Some, including More, held that church law prohibited divorce. He could not pledge himself to support any issue of a union he deemed to be illegal. In 1534 he was confined in the Tower of London for high treason and Elizabeth, the child of Anne, grew up to be England's great queen. In 1535, More was led to the scaffold and beheaded.

More was a great student. He wrote "Utopia" in Latin. He had doubtless read Plato and wished to convey this fact in the cryptic style so frequently employed in those far-away days. He causes his hero, Raphael Hythloday, to be introduced by a minor character in the following words of praise: ". . . . he hath sailed indeed, not as the mariner Palinure, but as the expert and prudent prince Ulysses; yea, rather as the ancient and sage philosopher Plato." By this we are left to judge that More's hero, the mariner Raphael, had the seamanship of a Palinure, the adventures of a Ulysses and the philosophy of Plato. Perhaps the use of the name Raphael is also intended to remind us of the angels.

Social Background of "Utopia"

Whether or not these allegories are intentional, the story of "Utopia" is Plato's "Republic" set to music. The mariner Raphael has journeyed to far-away places, taking first as his guide the great Amerigo Vespucci. But this intrepid explorer leaves Raphael at his own behest in a far strange land. Not content with that, Raphael journeys ever farther west, crosses deserts, comes at last again to civilized people. And there, taking ship, he makes his way to the Island of Utopia, wherein a socialist paradise is in full bloom.

The burden of More's argument, put in the mouth of Raphael, is that civilization as it exists in the 16th century is full of wars and thieves. Further, it appears that the one breeds the other. Soldiers come back from conflict and cannot find work. They turn to robbery. There isn't enough work for everyone anyway. This is because the governments of the civilized nations are pre-occupied with war, rather than with enterprise. Thus, armies disbanded result in thievery.

But, it seems, the reverse is true. Where does the king go to recruit his army? True, there are knights and nobles. But the vanguard is made up of men who are not gainfully employed. And no king can fight a war until he has sufficient of this type of man to call upon. Hence, the number of thieves in a nation determines to a degree the size of the armies soon to be mobilized. It is a vicious circle.

Obviously, says Sir Thomas, one must expect the government to solve the problem. And in far Utopia, an island of about 500 miles circumference, there are 54 cities. The entire area is organized and all work supervised and run by a powerful and "Godly government. . . . . .(with) all the good laws and orders of the same Island." Everything is governed. There is neither room nor time for freedom.

There is no need to discourse further on the details of the Utopian paradise. It is all that Plato could have wished. There are no thieves. There is no idleness. There is no private property. There is only beautiful, symmetrical, total government organization.

Whether More intended to be taken seriously or not, is open to question. At the end of his fantasy he appends a purported testimonial from one Peter Giles, citizen of Antwerp, who is part of the story and who attests that with his own ears he also heard the story from that peer of mariners, Raphael Hythloday. The first part of the testimonial is significant: "Thomas More, the singular ornament of this our age, as you yourself can witness, to whom he is perfectly well known, sent unto me this other day the 'Island of Utopia,' to very few as yet known, but most worthy; which, as far excelling Plato's commonwealth, all people should be willing to know. . . ." etc., etc.

Plato's influence was, indeed, profound and lasting, and More's impingement on the public mind only slightly less.

The word "utopia," coined by More, finds Webster including it as meaning: "any place of ideal perfection; also an impractical scheme of social regeneration."

And it is entirely possible that Samuel Coleridge, in writing "The Ancient Mariner," had the intrepid mariner Raphael in mind.

Arthur E. Morgan has done a study ("How Inca Socialism Came to North America," published in 1946) in which he conjectures that socialism flowered first in Peru, and that Raphael Hythloday, the leading figure of More's "Utopia," was actually a real person and not a fictional character. According to Morgan, Raphael's Utopia was in fact Peru and the story related to More an honest recitation of fact. Morgan suggests that the Incas discovered socialism, transmitted it to Raphael, who transmitted it to More, who transmitted it to many, including Edward Bellamy, whose romance is our next point of reference. That there is similarity between the Inca civilization, More's "Utopia" and other collectivist ideas to follow is unquestioned. It is also true that the Incas'

Peruvian political format, which developed between the years 1100 and 1540 in South America, is similar to Plato's conception.

We do not know from where the Inca rulers came. We only know that a system of absolute socialism was established which has been listed by Louis Baudin and Lewis Spence as being a socialist masterpiece. Baudin gives us "L'Empire Socialiste des Inka," and Spence in his "Myths of Mexico and Peru" shows us the connection between the Platonic master plan and the Peruvian reality.

"The Inca was the direct representative of the sun upon earth" (man of gold?), "the head of a socio-religious edifice intricate and highly organized. This colossal bureaucracy had ramifications into the very homes of the people. The Inca was represented in the provinces by governors of the blood royal. Officials were placed above ten thousand families, a thousand families, and even ten families, upon the principle that the rays of the sun enter everywhere, and therefore the light of the Inca must penetrate to every corner of the empire." (Could these blood-royal princes be men of silver?)

"There was no such thing as personal freedom. Every man, woman and child was numbered, branded, and under surveillance as much as were the llamas in the royal herds. Individual effort or enterprise was unheard of. Some writers have stated that a system of state socialism obtained in Peru. If so, then state surveillance in Central Russia might also be branded as socialism." (!!)

"A man's life was planned for him by the authorities from the age of five years and even the woman whom he was to marry was selected for him by the government officials. The age at which the people should marry was fixed at not earlier than twenty-four years for a man and eighteen for a woman. Colored ribbons worn around the head indicated the place of a person's birth or the province to which he belonged."

There are parallels between the Incas' savagely maintained equality and Plato's "Republic," but who wishes to attest that the Inca people are ancient Greeks or Egyptians who, knowing Platonic theory, threaded their way across the misty fastness of a possible Atlantis to Peru, there to act out the theory? It is possible, of course. But it is at least as possible and surely more believable that socialism is one of these persistent myth forms such as creation myths, hero myths, rain and thunder myths, etc., which seem to bear such close resemblance to each other, and yet spring from totally dissimilar soils to blossom and flourish amid people entirely unrelated and disassociated.

In any case, Morgan's effort was to trace the similarity of Incan socialism to modern times, an effort which is valuable. Our only problem here is that socialism has extensive origins which predate the Peruvian "golden" age by at least two thousand if not four or five thousand years. Consequently, we cannot agree that socialism originated in South America. Nor can we accept without question the Morgan point of view that More was so honest and forthright a man that he hesitated setting down the adventures of Raphael as fact and therefore colored "Utopia" and turned it into a fictional account. On the contrary, there is no evidence in "Utopia" that it was intended to be taken as fiction, although More must have known that the fantasy was unbelievable and would be so classed. Still, he takes what precautions he can and recites the story as a first-hand, historical treatise, appending to it an affidavit as to its authenticity.

The point is that socialism is not some recently evolved scheme of Karl Marx. It is a well-established doctrine that has had advocates in every tongue for at least fifty centuries.

Problem of Implementation

A secondary point is the natural dilemma of these planners of human life. How can one bring about a utopian paradise? The dream is a common one. But how does one implement the dream? Plato imagined that the parents of children might cooperate, if only the parents were sufficiently philosophical. But More makes no such protestation. Quite frankly, he doesn't even approach the problem. He gives us a science-fiction background and provides an island so far a-way that no one knows where it is. The island is discovered in full bloom. There is no transition necessary from More's

England to Raphael's Utopia. Like most of socialism, it makes a pleasant fiction, and the more fictional it remains, the greater the pleasure.

Let us provide one more illustration. Edward Bellamy is the author, the title of his book, "Looking Backward." It was published in 1888, only forty years after the print of the Communist Manifesto had dried. And again a debt is paid to the immortal Plato, whose dream of perfection via government control of the means of production and distribution is made manifest this time in a flowery romance.

Julian West is the hero, a scion of an old Boston family of stability and minor prominence. He has difficulty in falling asleep. A doctor named Pillsbury is called in on occasion to lull Julian into the arms of Morpheus by means of hypnosis. And to take full advantage of this trance, Julian has had built a special sound-proof room in which to enjoy his hypnotic slumber.

Unfortunately, one night after he has been mesmerized in his bed, the house burns down. Everything burns except the sound-proofed vault in which the hero lies. Someway, the room is overlooked in the debris, and time passes. The next thing Julian knows, he awakens with people in the room with him. It is the year 2000. He has slept from 1887, a period of one hundred and thirteen years, three months and eleven days.

While he slept, the world has changed. He awakens in a socialist utopia, reminiscent in all details of More's extravaganza and Plato's sophism. The bulk of the novel contains the breath-taking experiences of Julian, who finds to his surprise that life has been perfected by government decree while he slept.

There is no competition and, of course, no important property is owned privately. All jobs are provided by the state. There is only a single store, to which all persons go when they wish to purchase anything. Apparently it is all right to own smaller items of property. But all means of production and distribution are owned by the state. This store is a wonder. All it has on its shelves are samples. You pick out the item you wish to buy; a sales person telephones a factory; by the time you get home the item has been delivered. There are no brand names, of course. A can of tomatoes is a can of tomatoes, isn't it?

Best of all, there is no money. All persons receive script, not as a result of their efforts but simply because they are alive. If they appear incapable of spending their script wisely, a government overseer is appointed to prevent any foolish choice.

A reviewer of "Looking Backward" as late as 1949 had this to say: "The main value of 'Looking Backward,' 2000-1887, lies in its credible presentation of a socialist Utopia, and the book has served to introduce many famous people to the theory of socialism. Bellamy was not merely a follower of Marx and other economists; he rationalized for himself the case for economic revolution. The prophecies he makes for the world of A.D. 2000 are sometimes strikingly shrewd, and his judgments made of modern society are pointed and witty. Bellamy's idea was to present the ideas of socialism, as he saw them, in a way which would appeal to a wide reading public, both of yesterday and today."

This is almost modern science fiction. It is time travel which precedes the great H. G. Wells and which parallels Jules Verne. Again we see the More characteristic. The dream of socialism is inaccessible. It is approached through a Rip Van Winkle slumber rather than by boat. But, because so many people harbor the suspicion that profits are an evil, this book found a welcoming audience which was both large and impressionable. One president of the United States (F.D. Roosevelt) considered this one of his favorite novels. The book is catalogued as a novel rather than as science-fiction, where it properly belongs. So important did the book seem to the four-time president of the U.S.A. that he wrote his own book predicting the advance of socialism in which he acknowledged his debt to Bellamy by entitling it, "Looking Forward."

As we look at socialism, we are amazed at the size and scope of the belief, the length of its endurance, the number and greatness of the men and women who have applauded and championed it as a sacred cause.

We see the seeds of socialist thought in the greatest of our philosophers and the greatest of our religions. It is planted in great and enduring literature. Let us see how governments have fared with this perennial dream of sharing.

It is too early to discuss the socialist program of government. Instead, let us begin by viewing the emergence of the political syllogism. Then we may discover how the ineffective dream of thousands of socialists was marshalled into a program which set about creating a socialist society.

CHAPTER 4

OBLIVION TO THE RIGHT

The length and breadth of the socialist concept is impressive. It is safe to say that a majority of the works in the English language which have appeared during the past several decades, contain traces of or references to socialism. It is difficult to find a work, either factual or fictional, which is entirely lacking in the doctrine of share-the-wealth; divide the property; control the people for their own good.

Thus far we have examined the philosophy of socialism. It remains for us to examine the implementation of socialism. What Christianity overlooks; what Plato evades by an educational approach; what More and Bellamy both despair of discovering, is a practical means of establishing socialism. The dream of socialism, if it is ever to be more than a dream, must be translated into reality. A bridge must be built from the never-never land of fantasy to the firm granite of fact.

Curiously, no practical program for the promotion of socialism was devised from the days of Plato until the 19th century. True, we have the evidence of the Inca civilization, but the genesis of it is lost. The Inca experiment sprang from seeds that are unknown and went down under the scythes of time and the swords of the Spanish conquistadores. While some would insist that it was the swords of the Spaniards rather than the erosion of father time that proved the nemesis of the Incans, the fact is ably illustrated by this and other incidents in history (e.g., Egyptian downfall after Joseph socialized the agriculture of that nation) that total socialist control as it is extended thru time, tends to sap the vigor of defensive preparations. Prescott suggests that the total control exercised over the populace by their rulers deprived the people of the will to resist. It is known that the Spaniards, though superior in arms, were an incredibly tiny force. Sheer weight of numbers could have driven them off, if a will to fight had existed in the populace.

The Inca civilization presents a composite picture in itself, without known relationship to the mainstream of socialist thought. It is possible that there are other instances, too. Myth forms have a way of recurring without notable continuity.

It is possible, of course, that the Inca settlements developed as a natural result of socialism, since all primitive societies are socialist in character at their beginnings. This is gravely doubted, however. Some freedom of intellect must have existed at some period to explain the advance out of the stone and bronze ages by these people. They had discovered superior methods of agricultural cultivation. They understood the manufacture of intricate ornaments. Their art forms were far advanced over stone and bronze age cultures.

What is more likely is that the Incan people arrived at a high plateau of development and were then re-enslaved, with personal property being taken from them for the "good" of their society, by some political process combined with religious fanaticism.

But we do not know what inspired the Inca rulers to deprive their people of freedom; what political forms they employed; what ruses and strategems they conceived to en-slave their populace. And it is with this process that we are concerned. For if the dreams of the socialists are to be ful-filled in the United States and in our own time, the means to accomplish this are of interest.

Mainstream of Thought

Let us revert to the mainstream of this thought as it washes against our own embankments. One of the mighty currents is contained in the Christian ethic of charity which was frequently misinterpreted with compulsive overtones.

Alas, church and state have not always been separate. And if we consider the socialist doctrine to be found in the early practice of Christianity, and the working relationship that existed between the church and the various kings, lords and emperors of Christendom, we can envisage the rudimentary growth of the tentacles of compulsion weaving through both church and state.

Perhaps this is what caused Edward Gibbon, in his "Decline and Fall of the Roman Empire," to declare: "The influence of the clergy, in an age of superstition, might be usefully employed to assert the rights of mankind; but so intimate is the connection between the throne and the altar, that the banner of the church has very seldom been seen on the side of the people."

So shocking was this bit of keen observation that Oliphant Smeaton, who reprinted all of Gibbon's notes and added observations of his own, provided a footnote for this comment: "Gibbon's remark here is wholly incorrect."

But customarily, socialism was unorganized, and, except at intervals, voluntary. Of course, in the 18th century there was Adam Weishaupt, who formulated a kind of doctrine in which he combined the symbols of the Masonic order with a sort of nihilistic creed. But the Illuminati were more a black magic cult than a realistic device for sharing the wealth. There were writers and dreamers by the score who argued that something should be done.

Three World Movements

Then, within a period of 50 years beginning in 1840, the three principal methods of attaining to a socialist super state were drafted, executed and became world movements. If 20th century anti-socialists rue their generation as being prone to collectivism, they might be grateful that they escaped the hazards of the 19th.

It is Pierre Joseph Proudhon of Bexancon, France, to whom goes the credit for the first concrete plan which embodied a method of attaining the socialist goal. Proudhon has been classed as a philosophical anarchist. He was not original, but he was orderly and logical. He was a student of Plato;

and he had among his precursors, William Godwin of England who wrote a famous socialist novel called "Caleb Williams" and who is himself frequently credited with being the father of anarchistic communism. It was Godwin who wrote and published in 1793, "Inquiry Concerning Political Justice," which was one of the first efforts after Sir Thomas More to criticize government for its eternal bickering and war-making, while people went hungry. Godwin wished to do away with governments entirely, not only because they made war, but because they were instruments for protection of a wealthy class and thus assisted in the impoverishment of others. Godwin deplored violence, either by government or by persons outside of government, thus giving the lie to those who insist on linking him with the violent Marxists. But he considered accumulation of property an act of violence. The worst form of tyranny, he explained, was marriage.

It was from this spring that Proudhon drank deeply. He emerged with "Qu'est-ce que la Propriete?" ("What Is Property?") dripping from his pen. This was a point that Plato had not thoroughly developed. And this omission was now exploited by Proudhon, who answered his own question by proclaiming: "Property is robbery." The publication hit the streets in 1840. This was followed by a pair of pamphlets in similar strain a year later. He was arrested and brought to trial for expressing revolutionary opinions but was acquitted. From then to the end of his life (1865), Proudhon was a proud exponent of socialist share-the-wealth philosophy.

The Encyclopedia Americana has this to say:

"He was the first to formulate the doctrines of philosophical anarchism; he maintained that property was unjustifiable, that labor only should give just claim to share in the product of labor, and that consequently rent and interest should not exist. He thus far agreed with the socialist doctrine of value, but he was neither a socialist nor a communist; because the state depended upon and protected property he claimed that the state must be destroyed; and that the proper basis of society was a voluntary contract between individuals."

Let us quarrel with the editors of "Americana" for their flat assertion that Proudhon was not a socialist. His views on property proclaim him to be one. His views on government announce his individualism. The combination of the socialist-economic, but individualist-political view is called anarchy. Proudhon is the father of anarchy.

His ideas took hold, suffered certain modifications and were then multiplied. The Russian Prince Kropotkin fanned the flames of revolution inherent in any idea of property reallocation. He suggested a world order which would bring universal peace after "the present system of class privilege and unjust distribution of the wealth produced by labor that creates and fosters crime" had been abolished.

But what Proudhon planted in the way of peaceful seed, became a violent whirlwind in the mind of the most vigorous anarchist of them all, Michael Bakunin.

It was Bakunin who saw one major point which Proudhon had merely hinted at. To eliminate government, the inveterate protector of private property, one must use more than subtle propaganda. The answer to the force of government, said Bakunin, was the force of non-government. Anarchists would do well to face the facts. Propaganda for education's sake was not enough. He introduced the "propaganda of action," by means of which terror could be employed as an education weapon and the fear of death sowed in the ranks of the politicians.

Bakunin, through planned violence, advanced the cause of anarchy with precipitate haste, and wrecked it, almost totally. Only in recent years, some pitiful remnants of the ancient order have crept from their dark hiding places, once more to proclaim weakly the Proudhon thesis, "Property is robbery." "Governments, in supporting property, are sustaining robbery." "To eliminate private ownership, the government must first be removed."

Let us hope that the modern anarchists, who dreadfully abuse the name and meaning of both individualism and liberty, do not fall victim to the lure of Bakunin's propaganda.

Propaganda by Action

A record of anarchistic excesses might be in order.

In 1878 there was an attempted assassination of Germany's Emperor William. There was an attempt upon the lives of the German princes in 1883.

In 1886, in Chicago, the attention of the world was riveted to Bakunin's propaganda by action. A bomb explosion in the Haymarket killed a number of persons. Seven arrests were made, all of persons known to be teaching anarchy. Four were sent to the gallows, two drew life sentences and one was imprisoned for 15 years. The evidence in this case was uncertain and after the emotional uproar had subsided, petitions were circulated to free the imprisoned three. It was never established beyond a point of doubt who threw the bomb.

But, bomb throwing continued, and such events were frequently traced to anarchist motivation.

In 1893 a bomb exploded in the French chamber of deputies in Paris and the thrower, Vaillant, was a well-known anarchist leader.

In 1894, President Carnot of France was assassinated.

In 1898, the Empress Elizabeth of Austria was assassinated.

King Humbert of Italy was assassinated in 1900.

President McKinley was killed by the anarchist Czolgosz, in an autumn shooting in the year 1901.

And King George of Greece was sent to his death by an anarchist plot on March 18, 1913.

There have been unconfirmed reports occasionally ever since. By the time World War I swept over the troubled human race, anarchists were depicted by cartoonists as black-bearded, bomb-carrying radicals with a universal hatred of mankind.

This was a blind alley, an unsuccessful epoch in the effort to enact Plato's "Republic." It was a tragedy of error heightened by the fact that there is much good in some of the anarchist doctrine. Economically, the anarchists perpetually come unglued. But the anarchists' writings in support of individualism are profound and beautiful. In Godwin and Proudhon, without the mutations provided by Kropotkin and

Bakunin, we find a strange and peace-loving sophistry. But whether we ascribe to the anarchist the calm and gentle philosophy of individualism, or the violent and destructive purpose of the overthrow of rule, by the use of force, we come up against a solid obstacle. The anarchist is a socialist with an individualist twist respecting government. His central purpose is to eliminate private ownership. His means to that end is to eliminate the one agency he views as the perpetual friend of private ownership, the government.

Because of its basic individualism, anarchism can be classed as the right flank of the socialist political front. It has never been successful. Nowhere is there evidence that some politician, in fear of anarchist bombs, disbanded his government and fled to the hills.

The left flank of the socialist movement is by far the most publicized and the best known.

CHAPTER 5

THUNDER ON THE LEFT

If we may credit Proudhon with being the father of philosophic anarchy, we must credit Karl Heinrich Marx with the paternity of modern socialism. Considering the vast number of socialist writers who have preceded and succeeded Marx, the mystery is why this obscure, difficult and truculent expositor should be considered as a parent of a philosophy to which he contributed little originality.

His debt to Plato, Godwin and Hegel needs no embroidery from this direction. Nonetheless, Marx is being cussed and discussed in nearly every clime and his influence appears to be growing rather than waning. It might serve a useful purpose to cast about to see if a reason for this astonishing ascendancy can be made to appear.

Marx Was a Jew

Marx was born in 1818 in Treves, Prussia. His father was a German Jew. And here, perhaps, we have the first clue to Karl's preeminence at least in the U.S., despite the fact that the elder Marx went over to Protestantism and had his family baptised in the Protestant church.

Since the early days of Christianity, a strong anti-Jewish movement has spread through much of the western world, even into these United States. At the outset, Christianity was little more than a Jewish sect, dedicated to the preservation of the Jewish law and subservient to it in all particulars. It was the labor of Paul which opened the Christian faith to

areas beyond the Jewish Talmud, and many were the theo-
logical and ideological battles which ensued over this presumed breach of the ancient Hebrew protocols. There is no
need to embellish this study with a recitation of the various
pogroms against the Jews which swept Europe and parts of
Asia like a black plague beginning before the catacombs were
widely in use, and culminating only recently in Hitlerian and
Khrushchevian purges.

As a result of these persecutions, there is a sensitivity
in many Jewish minds respecting any type of criticism.
Matching this, in some non-Jewish circles, is an equally
tenacious brand of antagonism, which finds the very mention
of a Jewish name something inimical to peace and safety.
Karl Marx was a Jew by birth. That was all the information
the anti-Jewish movements needed to prove to them that
socialism was a dangerous and subversive doctrine. The fact
that there were hundreds of able socialists, beginning with
Plato, who preceded Marx, carried no weight with them then
and fails to impress them now.

Understandably, many Jews arose to defend Marx, not necessarily because they were socialists but because Marx was, or had been Jewish. There is nothing quite so conducive to vigorous propaganda as a violated religious tenet. Marxian socialism (communism) was classed in thousands of minds as a Jewish plot. The animosity between Jews and anti-Jews was carried to ferocious lengths, and has resulted in any number of wild and unfounded suppositions concerning Jews, anti-Jews, Christianity, socialism, communism and a score of other beliefs and dogma.

Marx thus became at once the best publicity device the socialists had ever found, and the socialists' most vulnerable Achilles' heel. If thousands of people learned about socialism through Marx's written efforts, it is equally true that thousands learned to hate socialism without even understanding what it was.

Some Jews, it seems, have never forgiven Jesus for not living up to what they expected from a messiah. Some Christians have never forgiven the Jews for crucifying the son of

God. In one of the strangest perversions of thought in the history of the world, socialism, which has roots in both Jewish Essene studies and the practices of the Christian apostles, is imagined in some quarters to emerge exclusively from Christianity and in other quarters from Judaism.

The fact that the earliest and best explanation of socialism was made by a Greek who was neither Jewish nor Christian seems to have escaped the emotional conclusions of the embattled theologians. This oversight has resulted in effective propaganda efforts on both sides of the religious front with the socialists sitting on the sidelines and chuckling merrily over the publicity gains contributed by non-socialists.

Karl Marx

Marx attended the German Universities at Bonn and Berlin and in 1841 received a degree of doctor of philosophy. He read Proudhon's studies of philosophical anarchism which first appeared in 1840, and in 1842 Marx's first published works launched the radical branch of socialism which is now called communism.

In the beginning he sided with Proudhon, but the anarchist's peaceful methods discouraged him. Proudhon had it that private ownership of property was a robbery, and that government, which protected private property, would have to be destroyed if private property was ever to be abolished.

Marx was a better politician. It seemed a shame to him to eliminate the single agency of force capable of wresting private property from the hands of the rightful owners. Why not, he reasoned, use government as the device to accomplish Proudhon's aims? And, to make certain that government remains tractable to the socialist command, he urged the formation of a vast army of proletariat, the working man. This working man, thru political democracy, could be counted upon to control the government; that is, the majority of persons in any country, inevitably the lowly proletariat, could be organized into shock troops, could place good socialists in office by means of the power inherent in sheer numbers, and the government, thus turned into a democratic institution, could seize "by degrees" all wealth owned by all private persons and firms.

The bridge from the dream of socialism into the hard reality of life appeared about to be translated into fact. This is the first step in the political syllogism of socialism. The theorists had their day. Now it was time for the practical men to step forward to claim the world.

"The Communists disdain to conceal their views and aims. They openly declare that their ends can be attained only by the forcible overthrow of all existing social conditions. Let the ruling classes tremble at a communist revolution. The proletarians have nothing to lose but their chains. They have a world to win. Working men of all countries, unite!" (Communist Manifesto, concluding paragraphs.)

In his rush to accomplish all things swiftly, Marx chose to ignore Plato's principal warning, namely, that democracy is the worst and most tyrannous of governments. Instead, Marx saw the use of democracy, majority vote, as the device he needed to bring about the very socialism that Plato had envisioned. Nor was he content to theorize along the line of action. He joined with Friedrich Engels, and the two of them formed the German Workers' Society, one of the first of the communist unions.

There is no doubt that Bakunin's thinking was colored to a large extent by Marx's revolutionary doctrine.

What is the substance of the Marxian doctrine? There are two principal themes that run through his enormous work, "Das Kapital," and his equally difficult and obtuse pamphlets and essays. In the first theme, Marx borrows heavily from the philosopher Hegel and establishes his dialectic materialism. In history, according to Plato and Hegel, the only true history is the history of ideas. Each idea as it first appears is true but is later matched with its own negation in a second idea. These two ideas meet head-on in conflict, from which ideological battle there emerges a third and superior idea which is a synthesis of the other two.

Dialectic Materialism

At this point, Marx departs from Hegel and presumes that what may be true for ideas is true for economics. He declares that there are two major economic forces, those of capital and those of labor. And to begin with, in all societies the capitalists have the best of it. They form an exploiting class and organize a government created in their own image. But they cannot succeed without the laboring class and herein are the thesis and the antithesis. The laboring class, the proletariat, to begin with have nothing but what the capitalists will give them in the way of subsistence. But as the proletarian class exists, it grows larger and stronger, until gradually it is more powerful than the capitalist class. Then, according to Marx, the inevitable action of history asserts itself.

The proletariat arises, smashes the government of the capitalists and establishes a democracy formed in the image of the working man. Marx sees this process as one inevitably filled with violence. He concludes that the rightful owners of property will not give up what they have without a struggle. The struggle will be violent, but the proletariat will always win!

Marx believed himself to be a materialist, but his faith in dialectic processes rather classifies him as a mystic. He conceives the universe as a "physical" mechanism, but he also supposes that it is ruled by mystic forces, or by an "inevitable destiny." He has it that economic forces control human beings, instead of viewing human beings as the active ingredient in creating economic forces. He sees environment, the physical and economic surroundings of the human animal, as the single dominating factor in man's existence. He does not discover that when environment, either physical or economic, is unpleasant and unrewarding to man, he will change it, or simply move away.

Thus, according to Marx, man is not active, but static, mastered by conditions. And the prescribed thesis-antithesis-synthesis process is inevitable and on an ascending scale. Ultimately, Marxian "good" will be found in the inescapable rise of a ruling class which will control all property and rule mankind totally.

This achievement ends history. The Marxian millenium endures unchanged on earth forever. This is because of the mystic economic forces which utterly master and control all men through their rulers. The international proletariat will become the human race.

The Marxian picture is translated, in fine, as being no more than "godless Christianity." The Communist Party has come to save mankind from the ceaseless conflict between God (history) and Satan (private ownership).

There are still savants who claim that Marx is scientific. Let us examine his science.

"In one word, you reproach us with intending to do away with your property. Precisely so; that is just what we intend." And again, "....the first step in the revolution by the working class, is to raise the proletariat to the position of ruling class, to win the battle of democracy.

"The proletariat will use its political supremacy to wrest, by degrees, all capital from the bourgeoisie, to centralize all instruments of production in the hands of the state, i.e., of the proletariat organized as the ruling class; and to increase the total of productive forces as rapidly as possible." (Communist Manifesto.)

Marx was, of course, striking out against the European mercantile system rather than against the American capitalistic system, with which he was hardly acquainted. His major error, sired by his collectivist convictions, has been correctly answered by the great Austrian economist, Ludwig von Mises, who presents the argument for **laissez-faire** capitalistic economy.

"Capitalism is essentially mass production to fill the needs of the masses. But Marx always labored under the deceptive conception that the workers are toiling for the sole benefit of an upper class of idle parasites. He did not see that the workers themselves consume by far the greater part of all the consumers' goods turned out. The millionaires consume an almost negligible part of what is called the national product. All branches of big business cater directly or indirectly to the needs of the common man. The luxury industries never develop beyond small-scale or medium-size units. The evolution of big business is in itself proof of the fact that the masses and not the nabobs are the main consumers. Those who deal with the phenomenon of big business under the rubric 'concentration of economic power' fail to realize that economic power is vested in the buying public on whose patronage the prosperity of the factories depends. In his capacity as buyer, the wage earner is the customer who is 'always right'." ("Theory and History," chapter 7.)

Surplus Value

The second theme of Marx relates to his theory of surplus value. In his first theme, he borrows from Hegel; in his second, from Ricardo. And this is Marx's effort to establish a moral premise for the violence he urges upon the world by the "inevitable" class struggle.

Surplus value, as Marx views it, always takes the form of interest, rent or profit. But anything in that form is essentially a robbery for all value in any article of production is contributed only by the laborer who worked to produce it. It is Marx's position that the laborer should receive the full return on every item he has produced. He will concede that management performs a necessary function and that function should be rewarded in a minor way. But he insists that property should not be permitted to earn of itself. Interest, a payment for the use of money; rent, a payment for the use of property; and profit, a payment for nothing at all, are immoral, according to him. He views "society" as the necessary beneficiary of all production. He holds that all profits must accrue to all society. And since society is to be served by the new democracy, rising like the phoenix from the ashes of the capitalistic ruins, then all workers must be viewed collectively; all production, collectively; all government, collectively; all capital, collectively. Production must be for use and not for profit. The hub of Marxian socialism is the government, which will obey the wishes of the proletariat and act as a holding company for all means of production and distribution.

Marx, in the third volume of his "Das Kapital," contradicts his first volume and suggests that in the end, with the elimination of the capitalist class, and hence the exploiting class, there will be no further need for government. What will emerge is a classless society. The means to accomplish this will be the removal of capitalists as exploiters and their replacement with proletariat exploiters and expropriators. But when these class distinctions have been wiped out by force, no such distinctions remaining, there will be no necessity for government, which is inevitably an exploiter. Here Marx was consciously making an effort to lure the anarchists into the communist camp. The anarchists saw thru the ruse and hooted him down.

The famous phrase, often attributed to Marx, that government will "wither away," belongs properly to Lenin.

Although both anarchists and communists are socialists, it is clear that anarchists are not communists, and communists are not anarchists. The common ground on which both stand is the elimination of private ownership. The anarchist imagines the procedure to be one in which government must be eliminated in order to bring about the desired end. The communist proclaims that the government shall be his tool in the process, and the organized labor movement shall be the **avant garde** of the process. But it is important to recognize that although Marx sought to change the form of government by force in order to bring about the utopia he envisaged, his central attack is leveled not at government, but at capitalists. His aim is the elimination of private ownership and the "overthrow of all existing **social conditions.**"

Only twice since the Marxian doctrines have been propounded have the communist devices for overthrowing a social order been employed on a gigantic scale. The first of these was in the Russian revolution and the second, in the Chinese.

We give priority to the Russian revolution because chronologically efforts to overthrow the long-established regime in Russia preceded any others on the planet so far as is known.

The first use of Marxian communist violence to destroy a government occurred in St. Petersburg in 1881, at which time a pair of bombs took the life of Czar Alexander II. The communists were not organized sufficiently to complete the political coup. However, from that date in 1881 until the successful overthrow of the czar in 1917, the Russian government was in a state of ferment and gains made by the socialists were constant and ultimately decisive.

The student of communist rebellion knows there were two revolutions in the same year, 1917. The first of these occurred in the first part of May establishing the Kerensky regime. The second rebellion occurred in October of 1917,[1] at which time Kerensky was forced to flee the country and Lenin assumed full power.

The second communist revolution of worldwide implication occurred in China beginning on October 10, 1911. The communist inspiration is not generally recognized because the leader of the rebellion, Sun Yat-sen, is remembered as the father of the Chinese republic. The use of the word republic in connection is misleading.

[1]Note: This second revolution, which we have called the October Revolution, actually occurred in November. The reason for the confusion in dates is that the Russians were behind in their calendar by two weeks. What occurred in October in Russia actually happened the first part of November so far as the rest of the world was concerned.

After the Boxer rebellion in 1900, Sun Yat-sen attempted to use the popular reaction as a means of establishing what he called a democratic government. The Manchu regime was overthrown and did not reappear.

Sun organized the Kuomintang, which was supposed to be a strong republican organization. Actually, it was socialist to the core.

A reactionary movement was started by the former viceroy, Yuan Shih-kai. Yuan attempted to assume the presidency of the republic for Sun, but it became apparent that Yuan planned to reinstitute the monarchy.

A second revolution occurred in 1913. In this second revolution Yuan was defeated and Sun was forced to flee to Japan. However, in 1917 Yuan died and Sun put himself at the head of a movement to establish an independent republic of South China.

Sun's socialist views assured him the support of the large mass of the workers in China, who did not understand the principles of private ownership. He was and still is idolized by the student class and the Kuomintang.

By 1923 Sun, having failed to set up a government along socialist-republican lines, called upon Russia for help. The Russian government, under Lenin, sent the agent Michael Borodin and General Galens to reorganize the government and the military force of Sun Yat-sen.

Two leaders arose at this time, both of whom had been trained in Moscow. One of them was General Chiang Kaishek; the other, General Mao Tse-tung.

Early in 1925, and shortly before Sun died, Chiang broke with the communist control of the Sun Yat-sen regime and attempted to establish a second reactionary movement, similar to that started earlier by Yuan, but essentially aimed at making himself president rather than emperor.

Chiang, through the scheming of communist and socialist elements throughout the world, including some within the confines of the American government, was finally maneuvered to a last island stronghold on Formosa, and Mao Tse-tung assumed the full leadership of the mainland of China, whereat the moment of writing he holds full power.

Thus, it can be said that the Russian revolution which began in 1881 came to a successful conclusion for the communist forces in 1917, and it can also be said that the Chinese revolution which began as a socialist-republican movement in 1911 under Sun Yat-sen, evolved finally as a full communist state under Mao Tse-tung.

We see that anarchy has never succeeded. Meanwhile, Marxian socialism has attained two major victories and possibly some minor ones. We are too close to many of these events to analyze them with objectivity. A hundred years or so from now, more accurate perspective could be obtained. Right now one could point to scores of places where Marxian ferment has begun which may or may not culminate in the establishment of a truly communist regime in a Marxian sense.

To focus attention upon these trouble spots would require careful observation of every Balkan country, every African region, every Central and South American nation, not to mention nations in the far east.

However, the Marxian violence is repugnant to most people, even to many strongly committed socialists. For every success it can claim, reaction has set in which is vigorous and potentially successful in the future. Anarchy and Marxism are the right and left flanks, respectively, of the socialist modus.

We will now examine the most successful and effective device put into use to bridge the gap between the socialist dream of economic equality and the facts of life.

CHAPTER 6

QUIET FLOWS THE RIVER

The third, and by far the most successful, attempt to bring Plato's socialist republic into tangible form was organized in London during the winter of 1883-84. The prime mover of the group was Edward R. Pease, a man contemporaries have largely overlooked in bestowing credit. Mr. Pease was the first secretary and historian of the Fabian Society and the socialist cause is indebted to him for his perseverance and dedication.

The announced aim of the Fabians was the "reconstructing (of) society in accordance with the highest moral possibilities." And since the socialists have inevitably taken the position that any amount of wealth held by one individual in excess of the wealth held by the other members of society constitutes a robbery, it is immediately apparent that the Fabians planned to further the socialist "moral" goal .... a redistribution of all wealth and property.

Collective Gradualism

This little group took the name of Quintus Fabius to be emblematic of their methods and called themselves "Fabian" as a result. It was this Roman general who was credited with the original use of guerrilla tactics against the Carthaginians in the Punic wars. He advocated a type of harassment whereby inferior forces could decimate superior forces on a gradual basis, without coming into direct and head-on pitched battles. This tactic appealed to the London socialists and Fabianism became both a part of their nomenclature and the central theme of the methods they sought to employ.

The Fabians agreed in most respects with Marx and with Proudhon. The economic aims of both these reformers are inherent in Fabianism.

The significant point of departure between Fabians and Marxians was simply this: Marx held that those who own property would never give up without a struggle and, therefore, violence would be an essential to bringing in the Utopian dream. The Fabians, on the other hand, believed that the property owners would be too stupid to know what was happening to them if the gradualism of Quintus Fabius was employed against them. Hence, the Fabians counselled gradual usurpation of the means of production and distribution, rather than a head-on clash between the capitalists and the proletariat. They believed the government would have to be changed to become responsive to the working classes. But instead of advocating Marxian revolution to accomplish this end, they championed the cause of evolution through the voting process.

Like Marx, they disagreed with Proudhon respecting the function of government. Government was the immediate tool of the Fabians. And here are the lines of demarcation which separate right, left and center of the socialist phalanx.

The rightists (anarchists) of the socialist entente maintain that governments cannot be used to advance the socialist cause, but rather that governments must be abolished as the first step toward victory.

The left flank (communist) holds that existing governments are capitalistic tools which must be overthrown and replaced by democratic forms. The democratic forms (permitting mass voting and majority decisions) will be the most useful tool of the socialist in bringing about a redistribution of wealth.

The Fabians (the center) are willing to accept any form of government in existence at any time, and by education (Plato's original proposal) and agitation along peaceful lines, subvert and alter the purpose of that government until it gradually becomes the effective tool of the socialists without any violent upheaval. Like Marx, they advocate the use of the trade union movement as the principal effective device to be employed toward the conversion of government into a socialist holding company.

Respectability

The Fabians immediately adopted two devices which had been barred to both of the radical extremes of the socialist front. They attracted a pair of well-known "names" to their letterhead, and they concentrated on accuracy and reliability in all of their written reports. The result of this sober and conservative approach to a revolutionary theme made them respectable. Never did they appear as revolutionaries. Instead, they masqueraded as a party seeking only to "do good" The government was the instrument of their crusade and total sharing was their goal. They did not seek to abolish politicians as Bakunin had done with the anarchistic cause. They did not seek to abolish a particular form of government as Marx had attempted, with the more or less hidden aim of forming a second government in keeping with their program. Rather, they immediately obtained prestige by joining in with the existing government, recognizing in it certain inherent socialistic tendencies. These they sought to enlarge and exploit by appealing to the public's general sense of charity on the one hand, and by causing capitalists themselves to experience a sense of guilt by reason of the very success they had had in their activities of production and distribution.

George Bernard Shaw, the eminent playwright, and a man of considerable force and wit, was immediately attracted to the movement and became one of its staunchest leaders. Sidney Webb, a successful office holder, became another of its leaders. His wife, Beatrice, is considered of equal or even greater influence. In the process of their expansion the Fabians also attracted such luminaries as the great Theosophist Annie Besant, and the redoubtable Henry George Wells.

The immediate aim of the Fabians was not to form a new political party but to permeate existing parties. Thoroughly grounded Fabians joined both conservative and liberal parties in England, particularly the latter, and were successful in obtaining office in popular elections. After awhile they became powerful enough to organize the present labour party, as there is a natural affinity between Fabian techniques and those employed by labor bosses. The Fabians also organized a research department which spent time and money in ferreting out instances of "capitalistic abuse." These instance were highlighted and pounced upon by other wings of the socialist cause.

Branches of the society were organized in America, where an infiltration of the Democratic Party immediately got underway. In recent years the Fabians have so successfully "permeated" both Democratic and Republican parties that to all practical purposes the aims of both embody scores of socialist objectives. So wholeheartedly has the American political front moved toward socialist objectives that the Socialist Party leader, Norman Thomas, was moved to announce that the disbanding of the Socialist Party in this country was in order since its major aims had already been achieved by the other and older political groups.

At one time, dedicated American Fabians were toying with the idea of forming an actual labor party in this country, patterned after the British socialist-labour group with its overt purpose of "nationalizing" the basic means of production and distribution. But the Fabian ideas have been so readily accepted and have expanded through the minds of so many people so rapidly that their circulation far out-stripped the processes of organized effort.

In a sense, the Fabians proved the logic of Kant and Hegel. The Fabian movement is, in a manner of speaking, the synthesis between the radical right and the radical left of the socialist pantheon. Having divorced violence from their framework, they caught the anti-socialists off guard and defenseless.

The free enterprise community has endeavored to organize against socialism. It took little in the way of such organization to defeat the propaganda by action of the violent Bakunin. However wrong and destructive a particular politician may appear to be, few people wish to see a blood bath with the heads of their government dropping into the basket at the base of the guillotine.

And to organize against political Marxism is relatively simple. All one has to do is to strengthen the existing form of government so that it can resist the attempts to destroy it by force and violence. Also, by employing the government as an intermediary in labor-management friction, the use of unions as the advance guard to bring on socialism through concerted revolutionary violence is effectively curtailed.

Both the right and the left flanks of socialism depend on violence, and violence is generally abhorrent to civilized men and women.

Difficulties of Meeting Fabian Attack

But here is shown the skill and the wisdom of the socialist middle ground. For the very attempts of the free enterprise community to strengthen government so that violence does not occur, either against the politicians themselves, or against any particular form of government, play right into the hands of the Fabians. For all governments, by reason of their aims and claims of justice, inevitably contain socialist concepts. And the larger and more vigorous any government becomes, the more thoroughly does it lean in the direction of Fabian victory.

Belatedly and in a few well-informed quarters in America, this is now recognized. But the great mass of American voters remain, at this date, almost totally innocent of such knowledge. Patriotic societies, the most ferocious enemies that socialism has ever inspired, fight heroically to stem the tide of anarchy and Marxism, only to find themselves in the very vanguard of the Fabians, helping enlarge government, to make it more formidable, to cause it to collect larger taxes, to instill greater regulations, to commit acts of regimentation and coercion, to intervene in the economy, and ultimately to move the means of production out of the hands of the private owners and collect such means in the hands of the political mechanism.

The strength of the socialist adversary, the free market itself, is the very strength employed by the Fabians. This could be called political ju jitsu.

Socialism is inevitably a parastic development. It has no strength of its own, but by employing political Fabianism it drains the energy from the private enterprisers and uses that energy to destroy enterprise. It is business cannibalism which, if followed long enough, will not only destroy free enterprise, but will finally consume the socialists as well. No parasite can exist without its host. And here is the most cruel development. For conservative efforts to maintain private ownership within the framework of the conservative point of view provide just sufficient leeway for the socialists to continue to gain power and to grow fat on the life-blood they drain away from their opponents.

With glee, the world socialist front capitalizes on this American tendency. Marxists in Russia pound the war drums and in America patriots urge greater appropriations for defense. The result is a vast movement of wealth and capital into governmental control and management, which is the economic aim of Marxists, anarchists and Fabians alike.

"Do good" societies are formed to decry the poverty of persons in certain segments of the nation's population. Humanitarians quickly rally to the socialist banner and the welfare state is born and made strong with the transfer of still greaten wealth into the hands of the government.

Tariffs and Subsidies

Social planners appear and seek to bolster certain types of enterprise at the expense of more successful or more profitable enterprises. Tariffs and subsidies, the twin knives employed in socialist in-fighting, are brought into play and again more wealth moves out of private hands and into the control of the state.

On the subject of tariffs, the question is particularly complex. At the moment (1960) there is an apparent socialist coup in the making which appears to be aimed at the elimination of tariffs; and as a counter to this move, conservatives of Republican stamp are vocal in demanding tariff protection against commodities manufactured in foreign lands.

This is an illustration of the trap into which conservatives fall. Seeking to protect themselves, they conclude that the socialist front favors freedom in this area and, consequently, rather than grapple with the principles involved, they simply turn about and advocate a position which at the moment appears to be a shrewd defensive move to protect the rights of private ownership, whereas it is actually socialistic. What conservatives are prone to overlook in the area of tariffs is that the socialist Fabians are not in the least interested in eliminating tariffs, although that is their first publicized step in the gradual process they invoke. On the contrary, socialists at the moment favor the elimination of NATIONAL tariffs, particularly in the United States, with the view to placing all trade under immediate international control through the United Nations, GATT, and other similar trade restricting treaties and agreements.

Thus, the socialist entente is urging a course of action which consists of two steps, not one. The first step is precarious for them, for if they managed to obtain the elimination of tariffs without an immediate placement of all international trade under international control, they would have substantially weakened their efforts to destroy private ownership. If a true atmosphere of free trade at international levels did pertain, private ownership would be enhanced.

Events indicate, on the basis of conservative reaction, that the move is risky but not in error, intellectually, for the vanguard of the anti-socialist opposition is taking the very stand the socialists counted on them to take. Should the conservatives, in the immediate future, abandon their insistence on a protective tariff, become imbued with the idea of total free trade, and stand by their guns, the socialists would have been ousted from a politically astute position and would find themselves floundering. They would have assisted the very condition they seek to eliminate: the right to own property privately. And then if they failed to win international control of all trade, the result would be a major gain for the anti-socialist free enterprisers.

Here, as in similar cases, the socialist front is counting on the stupidity of capitalists, generally; the willingness to take a short-term, rather than a long-term position; the failure of the free enterprise community to fight for a principle, rather than for what is made to appear as an immediate dollar gain.

It is almost predictable that the free enterprisers will take the position which is philosophically and politically in error and thus hasten their own undoing at the hands of some international government cabal. Socialists are confident this will prove to be the case.

Meanwhile, under the supposition that "capitalism is outmoded," the state itself becomes an enterpriser, using tax money wrested from citizens as the capital by means of which it sets up hundreds of business which compete, in a tax-exempt status, against tax-paying enterprises. Land, the precious commodity on which all of us depend, drifts back into state ownership by means of military seizure and eminent domain. It is possible by virtue of extensive insured loans placed upon millions of homes by government agencies that, ultimately, in the midst of financial crisis the government could foreclose. Ironically, the idealistic professors of our schools and colleges, indoctrinated with huge helpings of Plato, agitate for more governmental aid to education, careless that with the aid goes inevitable political control. The dream of Plato stands close to fulfillment in America at the hands of Fabian gradualism. The income tax, the coercive draft, the United Nations, its endless agencies, schools and colleges, and hundreds of thousands of private clubs and organizations, carry forward the Fabian theme.

Fabianism Is Winning

In candor, the Fabians have the upper hand. Only in isolated pockets is there resistance to the tidal wave of socialist persuasion. And what is true in America is even more strikingly evident in England, France, Spain, Italy, the Middle East, India, the Benelux countries, Sweden, South America, Africa, New Zealand and Australia, and of course in China and Russia. Name any country. The chances are its government is predominantly dedicated to socialist concepts.

Individualism, the true opposite of socialism, is in disrepute the world over.

It may be true that strong government provides the answer to anarchy. It may be true that patriotism provides the answer to Marxism. But until something can be done to provide the answer to Fabianism, the cause of individualism is lost.

This is the reason for perplexity and confusion in the minds of conservative businessmen. They have long advocated government in place of anarchy. They have long upheld patriotism in place of Marxian violence and subversion. But how can the businessmen oppose socialism, when political action, legal force, defense preparations, and even their churches, schools, and clubs advance the socialist cause day after day?

Let us be completely frank with ourselves. If there is even a residue of opposition to the socialist front, credit must be given not to individualists but to the nature of things as they are. Do what they will, and the socialists are in the seats of the mighty and thus capable of doing what they please, they inevitably come up against the hard facts of reality. If they are deterred, it is not through the brilliance of the individuals who have opposed them. Rather, it is that nature and life are arrayed against them.

Even if individualism as a doctrine should be lost; if there were no such thing as an articulate opposition to the socialist creed; if every government and every human being consciously embraced the collectivist objectives, still those objectives would fail.

This is the reason our civilization has not already been swept to oblivion. Despite ourselves, the laws of nature and of life continue to function. Socialists may make up the largest team but it is inevitably the losing team.

If Hegel's rules of logic apply to the socialist conception, there is no reason the same rules cannot be made to apply to the individualistic position. It is time for a synthesis in the anti-socialist camp, wherein the proper intelligent means for opposing intellectual (Fabian) socialism can be applied.

What must be found is a philosophy of thought which will avoid the political trap of the Fabians in which, while Marxism is opposed, private ownership is undermined. Clearly, no direct political means will suffice, because direct political means result in increasing and magnifying the importance of government, thereby advancing the Fabian objective. But it may be possible, through means which will have an indirect political repercussion, to bring about the denouement of the entire socialist structure.

CHAPTER 7

NATURE'S LOGIC

In prior chapters the origins of socialism were marshalled. The roll call was not exhaustive, nor is it necessary for our purposes to make it so. Our purpose is not to count and classify each tuft of moss in the collectivist bog, but rather to locate the general whereabouts of the bog, and if possible to discover why men persist in wandering in such difficult and unrewarding terrain.

We are confronted immediately by the startling — even shocking — fact that the bog has very ancient origins and that it lies about us on every side. Only occasional islands in the sea of marsh give us assurance that there could be something better than the dismal swamp of universal shirk-and-share.

So, let us begin with these non-utopian islands. The first fact to confront us here is that the islands are natural conditions which have occurred when men followed their own natures and acted in accordance with their own best interests. The bog has occurred when men have become fog-bound in the miasma of illusion and suppose the world to be other than it is.

Early Socialist Colonies

Clearly, then, our first requirement is to determine something of the nature of man and the world in which he lives. And here we must confine ourselves to stark realism. Let us not seek to ascertain the nature of man on the basis of what we hope his nature should be. Let us not have a theory and then seek to fit man into it. Let us insist on accurate observation, without bias in any direction, and be content with our findings, sans theory.

Admittedly, there is an almost universal dream of share-the-wealth. This is an observable fact. It has been catalogued in prior pages. It is also observable that an actual condition of share-the-wealth has never in the history of man been maintained. Colonies of share-the-wealthers have been founded from time to time. Our own country, America, has had a number of them. The Plymouth colony, with its Mayflower Compact, was a commune. It constituted a "planned economy" in which all means of production and distribution were to be controlled by the central authority.

While the colonists were still aboard the vessel which brought them to the bleak New England coast, they agreed to be bound to a central authority "for our better ordering and preservation and furtherance of such just and equall laws, ordinances, acts, constitutions, and offices, from time to time, as shall be thought most meete and convenient for the generall good of the Colonie unto which we promise all due submission and obedience."

It was understood immediately, even before land came into view, that no man could strike out for himself; that all produce to be raised or all provender discovered should belong not to the finder or producer but to the collective; that all colonists would share and share alike and that any deviation from this code would be met with the most severe punishment.

A reading of Governor Bradford's history of the colony is instructive. After two disastrous winters and a single summer in which a pitiful harvest was all that rewarded the conscript efforts of the settlers; after robbery and thievery had become common; after sickness and death from exposure and malnutrition had reduced the colony numerically and close to despair, Governor Bradford proclaimed that he would no longer lead the colony according to the agreement of the Compact. He allotted to each man his own land and told him to work for himself if he would; that all he could produce would be his but that anything he failed to produce would simply add to his own discomfort.

With astonishing vigor, heretofore lacking, men and women and little children applied themselves to their fields. The harvest this time was so plentiful that the first Thanksgiving banquet to be held in the new world was celebrated on the shores of Massachusetts Bay.

It is noteworthy that the Plymouth colonists were devout Christians and had only tried to establish a divine economic scheme on earth. They found the facts of life are such that a compulsive mutual sharing is not conducive to production. When they abandoned that procedure and undertook to establish an independent and an individualistic economy, there was not only enough but "to spare." The colonists learned to trade their personal surpluses with the surpluses of others and from that moment, the adventure succeeded.

But the Plymouth colony was only one of the efforts to socialize the economy in this nation; it was certainly not the most important, nor was it either last or first.

James Truslow Adams reminds us that the Virginia colony (founded 1607) had an experiment in socialism. Captain John Smith commented: "When our people were fed out of the common store, and labored jointly together, glad was he (who) could slip from his labour or slumber over his taske, he cared not how; nay, the most honest among them would hardly take so much true paine in a weeke, as now for themselves they will doe in a day; neither cared they for the increase presuming that howsoever the harvest prospered, the general store must maintain them, so that wee reaped not so much corne from the labours of thirtie as now three or four do provide for themselves." But this, of course, came after Captain Smith's dictum: "Those who will not work, shall not eat!"

And as John Rolfe wrote: "They could sit under their own fig tree in safety, gathering and reaping the fruits of their labors with much joy and comfort," after the transition from a socialist to an individualist economy had occurred.

In 1825, Robert Owen founded a socialist society at New Harmony, Indiana. It is interesting to note that it was this American who, according to the Encyclopaedia Britannica, ninth edition, gave us the word "socialism." The theories of Owen were originally called "Owenism" but this was unpopular with many of his followers. It is believed that the words "socialist" and "socialism" were first used by Owen in discussions in England in 1835. The term "socialist" was also used in France in 1838 by Pierre Leroux, and figured in 1839 in Reybaud's "Socialistes Modernes." Marx and others from 1840 on, also used the term.

Francois Fourier organized a number of communes in this country and the arguments of Fourier so inspired the great newspaperman and educator, Horace Greeley, that the town of Greeley was established in the State of Colorado under the aegis of the Fourier phalanx. There were additionally, the Oneida colony in upstate New York, the Amana colony in mid-Iowa, and by far the most famous, Brook Farm, established in 1841 at West Roxbury, Massachusetts, with such illustrious "transcendentalists" vitally concerned with its success as Ralph Waldo Emerson.

Without exception, these colonies have all succumbed to the realities of life as it is. The "share-the-work" and "share-the-reward" theories of these movements, largely inspired from religious doctrine, have come to naught.

The most successful of all was the above-named Amana colony. This particular group of Christian devotees labored so diligently that they maintained their socialistic integrity from 1855 until approximately 1932, having been in existence as a going concern for more than 75 years. The descendants of the original settlers at that time took stock of their affairs. They found that their Amana blankets were superior products; that Amana refrigerators and freezers were in great demand; that they were missing out by virtue of their socialistic methods since they were not competing on a PROFIT basis with the other enterprises in the nation. They reorganized, divided the property of the colony among the heirs and workers, formed a cooperative of 1,400 members, and abandoned the strict commune idea. Since then, the members of the colony have been permitted to profit personally by virtue of their efforts and there is little indication at the moment that the reorganization has been much in error.

Had the shift been all the way — had the Amana people consented to the formation of a true stock company and abandoned even the collectivist features which persist in a marginal manner in cooperatives — their success would have been assured. As it now is, though they have a tax advantage because of their cooperative character, they are still unable to compete most effectively since individualistic profit isn't possible. Thus, they cannot offer the incentives to the individuals of true genius that may arise. Consequently, there will be a tendency for the colony to drift along at status quo, until such time as a further reorganization comes, or until such time as free competition from outside reduces it to stagnation and ultimate dissolution.

Nonetheless, the Amana colony deserves a pat on the back as the longest to be sustained, unnatural community ever to endure on North American soil. Its existence under modified capitalism establishes it as a freak of nature, not as a going concern. And it might be pointed out that the standard of living of the inhabitants prior to 1932 was so low that it failed utterly to attract new followers and had become ingrown and psychologically cannibalistic to the ambitions and desires of its weary devotees. Even now, its standards cannot be favorably compared with those of a majority of the citizens in nearby Cedar Rapids. Amana wins the prize for submissive endurance of its inhabitants, not for freedom and daring.

It would be unprofitable and a useless repetition to attempt to catalogue all such socialistic communal efforts even in this nation, let alone the rest of the civilized world. Hope springs eternal. In truth, scarcely a year goes by but some economic fanatic, inwardly urged to "do good," appears with a handful of followers and attempts to establish a commune. It is predictable that they will all fail sooner or later. Most will fail sooner. This is not the way of the world, nor is it within the nature of man. To their credit, let it be noted that most of these colonizing efforts on the part of good and idealistic men and women are conducted without the use of brute force.

The real test of modern socialism will not be found in the framework of a voluntary association. It will be found in the involuntary association ordained by an instrument of force, a government.

To discover examples of governmental inauguration of socialist ideas requires no search at all. All governments, both modern and ancient, have endorsed socialism to some degree. But for a precise example of how socialism advances upon a people by means of their government, we can think of no better than that furnished by the government of the United States.

If ever a government was established with the principles of individualism predominant in the minds of its founders, the American form of government provides us with the case in point. And this illustration will be employed shortly so that the political syllogism of individualism as contrasted with that of socialism can best be observed.

American Advantages

What is important for us to recognize in this chapter is that the nature of man is opposed to collectivism and favorable to individualism. That is why, in this country, with a government originally dedicated to individualism and independence, man's lot improved so swiftly and with such startling results.

Once the individualism of this nation had been secured, largely by virtue of the Declaration of Independence and its inspired utterance of the rights of man, inventive genius came to the fore here as in no other place on earth.

When Sargon I ordered his Assyrians into battle twenty centuries before Christ, the favored captains rode in chariots and the leaders of units rode in saddles. The horse was the king of battles.

When Washington commanded his troops in the battle of New York, the progress of nearly 4,000 years had put an extra pair of iron-shod wheels on the chariot and the general himself rode in a saddle.

Today, thanks to the freedom and the individualism of our primary economy, Americans ride farther and faster on the seat of their pants than any other people in any time or place. We have trains and automobiles and steamboats, and airplanes and rocket ships and even the lowly motorcycle and bicycle. Any one of these things would have been looked upon as a divine manifestation by Sargon I.

For thousands of years, men lived in pitiful hovels and caves, shivering in the cold, coughing and inhaling the smoke from inadequate wood and coal fires. Now they live in three-bedroom homes of taste and comfort; in steam-heated apartments of luxury and refinement; or in hotels which put to shame the loftiest platforms of the Babylonian Ziggurat. They have centralized, diffused heating furnished by coal, oil, gas or electricity. They have, with the flip of a switch, the intrusion of the light of day into the darkest hours. They even have air-conditioned comfort in sultry mid-summer. They shut out the vicissitudes and rigors of the temperatures both hot and cold, and apply themselves in whatever manner is pleasing to them.

From the pallet of damp and vermin-infested straw, modern man has graduated to down filled, inner spring luxury. From the rude stone or wooden bench, he reclines gracefully on foam rubber, covered with a myriad of velours, brocades and plastics.

From a diet of half-raw mutton, acorns and the inner bark of trees, with occasional bread made from flour so full of grit that it ruined his teeth, man has moved up the scale of elegance to the point where the average regularly employed worker in these United States dines at a table covered either with linen or with highly decorative individual place mats, uses sparkling glassware and stainless cutlery, and affords a menu that would have sent the kings and emperors of a few hundred years ago into spasms of envy. He has his choice of a dozen kinds of bread, plus rolls, all grit free; he has an assortment of canned goods so vast that there is no one in the United States today who can, without prompting, tick off the delicacies available to him for a few pennies.

So far has he gone that he now believes that salads, the indescribable luxury of Saladin, are an essential to the well-planned meal. His steaks, roasts, chops and cutlets are stuffed into his personal deep freeze unit in such array that he could feed a platoon of men with little warning and probably without bankrupting himself.

And as for vegetables, he has such a plethora of beans, cabbages, squash, pumpkins, lettuce, peppers, potatoes, rice, tomatoes, lentils, sprouts, cauliflower, onions, radishes, beets, carrots, parsnips, rutabagas, broccoli, chard, spinach, zucchini, oats, barley and okra that he himself doesn't know what to do with it all. And as for fruits, melons and berries, there is no limit to what he can have in or out of season.

Instead of having a sizable portion of our society drop dead from starvation as an annual event, the American **mal de tempus** is heart trouble, much of it occasioned by over-eating!

And the clothing! In the 17th century it was not uncommon for an individual to receive a single garment at maturity which garment was to suffice for his entire life. Changes of linen were afforded only by the nobility and royalty, which had taxes to sustain its taste. Now, in America, and beginning to splash over to the rest of the world, is such an array of clothing as to stun the imaginations of a Belshazzar, a Cheops or a Richard I. We dress not entirely from necessity, but from sheer joy. The hues of our donnings put the rainbow to shame. And as for warmth in the cold, and coolness in the heat, who in the time of France's Louis XIV could have imagined such comfort?

Take one other thing, the cleanliness. Human beings during what we call the dark ages washed when they were rained on. Otherwise, once a year ALL OVER was enough. A few fanatics insisted that four annual ablutions were in order, one to celebrate the beginning of each season of the year! But such extravagance was out of reach for most.

Now we are born into antiseptic purity with a bar of soap and running hot water only a few steps away. We have shower baths and tubs at such frequent intervals that no modern home would be complete without at least one such advantage.

But these things, and thousands more, came into common usage in these United States not because our government caused it, but because our government was unable to prevent it! All the improvements were made by individual men in an individualistic economy the like of which had never been seen before.

It was not that other people in other places were not hungry, and tired, and dirty, and poorly clad, and destitute of reasonable shelter. It was that their governments had practiced socialism for so long, that such INDIVIDUAL advantages were forever out of reach of the ordinary citizen.

Socialism Was Ordinary

Don't imagine that socialism is peculiar to our time and place. Rose Wilder Lane, in her great book, "Discovery of Freedom," reminds us of the facts. She quotes from Henry Thomas Buckle's book, "History of Civilization in England," to give us an insight into conditions in England and in France before the industrial revolution.

"In every quarter, and at every moment, the hand of government was felt. Duties on importation, and on exportation; bounties to raise up a losing trade, and taxes to pull down a remunerative one; this branch of industry forbidden, and that branch of industry encouraged; one article of commerce must not be grown because it was grown in the colonies;

another article might be grown and bought, but not sold again, while a third article might be bought, and sold, but not leave the country.

"Then, too, we find laws to regulate wages; laws to regulate prices; laws to regulate the interest on money; custom-house arrangements of the most vexatious kind, aided by a complicated scheme which was very well called the sliding scale — a scheme of such perverse ingenuity that duties varied on the same article, and no man could calculate beforehand what he would have to pay.

"To this uncertainty, itself the bane of all commerce, there was added a severity of exaction, felt by every class of producers and consumers. The tolls were so onerous, as often to double and quadruple the cost of production. A system was organized, and strictly enforced, of interference with markets, interference with manufactures, interference with machinery, interference even with shops.

"The ports swarmed with tide-waiters, whose sole business was to inspect nearly every process of domestic industry, to peer into every package, and tax every article; while, that absurdity might be carried to its extreme height, a large part of all this was by way of protection; that is to say, the money was avowedly raised, and the inconveniences suffered, not for the use of government, but for the benefit of the people. In other words, the industrious were robbed in order that industry might thrive.

"Indeed, the extent to which the government classes have interfered, and the mischiefs which that interference has produced, are so remarkable as to make thoughtful minds wonder how civilization could advance in the face of such repeated obstacles. In some of the European countries the obstacles have, in fact, proved insuperable, and the national progress is thereby stopped."

Be it remarked that all of these "benefits" to human beings hampered them, and in contrast, when Americans on these far shores were left free of the "protection" furnished in such excess, they ran up the curtain on a new age of plenty, vouchsafed them by reason of an individualistic economy. By abolishing state tariff restrictions, the American scene became the largest free trade area in the world. By having a feeble and limited government, the individual man received the scepter of his own economic prowess and exploited it, to his own advantage, but to everyone else's as well.

Surely, it must be seen that any system of economics which can produce such abundance is manifestly superior to prior economic systems which, while seeking to protect and to cause a sharing of burdens, penalized the productive and created an almost universal poverty. And such a benevolent system must be natural, one in harmony with the facts of life as they are. It cannot be contrary to nature, for if it were, no such results could have been forthcoming.

Socialist Failures Recur

Thus the socialists are given the lie. Socialism has had centuries in which to prove itself. Its failures are staggering. Individualistic enterprise, as a general policy, has had only a few years of freedom. Yet in those years, the whole complexion of human life has been changed for the better. How can anyone imagine the human race would be benefited by reversion to the collectivized failures of hundreds of nations and thousands of years of experience, when the clear and certain success of unhampered freedom of enterprise has been proved to be correct and has demonstrated its fertility, its productivity, its precedent-shattering benefits?

But now, it appears, thanks to the manifold promotions of the socialist complex through governmental, educational and religious channels, we are turning our backs on a natural and productive order to embrace the planned economic state.

It may be we are near a socialist apex now. Similar conditions have existed before and were preludes to disasters. It is as though nature will permit violations of her fundamental laws up to a point. Then, she rises up, shakes out her skirts and puts the erring nation in order. Such order as an outraged nature can enforce may compel a temporary reversion to more primitive economies.

The Individualist Ethic

We began with the nature of the world as the socialist sees it — a whirling spheroid with fixed amounts of land and water and a population which, in the socialist moral clime, should share the land and the benefits to be derived from either land or water on an equal basis. The individualist recognizes the more or less static ratio of land to water; the differences between one parcel of land and all other parcels whatsoever; and the divergencies in human character, personality, skills, talents, inclinations and proclivities which among people are so vast as by contrast to give all land and water a universal sameness.

Additionally, the individualist recognizes there is no such thing as a stable and constant population. While the land mass may remain more or less a constant, human life does not. The population of the earth is expanding. But if we rely on socialist persuasion and conceive of division as the moral absolute, then it must follow that each new birth is a disaster. Each additional person must be inserted in the equation for ultimate sharing with the total wealth. The more people alive, the smaller the share each will finally have. Socialism becomes an open doorway to universally shared poverty with state birth control as the only means of preventing universal starvation.

The socialist must, perforce, recognize the inequality of land values and in human abilities. Also, he must recognize that a growing population forever dislocates a static absolute, even in his idealistic static dream world. The socialist doesn't approve of the world as it is. He recognizes that he cannot change it in its beginnings, so he attempts to harness all divergent elements and by force to bring about uniformity at the end.

He subscribes, sometimes unconsciously, to the theory of Thomas Malthus that the world population can never be greater than the food supply and that whereas food supplies tend to increase on an arithmetical basis, populations tend to increase on a geometric basis. Hence, as with everything else, he concludes that populations must be controlled and fall under the purview of an almighty state.

On the contrary, the individualist sees the nature of the world to be diversified; recognizes the diversity of human beings; concludes that the products of these diversified elements will always be diversified, adjusts himself to the reality and is happy in the result. The individualist stops worrying about conditions which he finds in nature. He knows that nature preceded him and that he is a product of it, as much a part of the universe as any other part of it. He will adjust himself to nature's law rather than seek to ignore it or to create fictions about it.

And for the theories of Thomas Malthus, he reserves the back of his hand. He may concede that the world's population will never be able to expand beyond its ability to eat. But he points to the tractor, the combine, the harvester, soil enrichment chemicals, selective plantings, scientific cultivation, etc., and offers evidence that the ability of human beings to produce food has increased so sharply during the days of America's free enterprise decades that it has actually provided for the population increase. Instead of always having the population

pressing against the food supply, as Malthus gloomily predicted, the individualist shows that the reverse, at least in
America, has been demonstrated when free individualistic enterprise is granted room to expand and to flourish. Now the
food supply in America is pressing against the people. A non-
Malthusian problem is where to put the produce. Granaries
have long since been full to bursting. Surpluses have been
stored in caves, in silos, and in the holds of ships going nowhere. Even city streets have been heaped high with grain,
because there was nowhere else to put it. It can be argued the
surplus came with political incentives. True. But is was human
energy and land and tools which produced the abundance.
Governments do not produce food. And what has been done
in America, only partly free, may be duplicated elsewhere if
socialism will be abandoned.

And here is perhaps the most important single rule to
be adopted in respect to nature. Nature may be harnessed,
but she will not be thwarted. She is harnessed by scientific
judo, a process wherein her great laws are directed in such

a way that they serve a human purpose. But her laws are not eliminated. Man may not reverse the infinite flow of nature's energies. Nature moves in understandable, predictable fashion. Man may study her moods and directions and ultimately comprehend them sufficiently to employ them gainfully. But he may not bid nature reverse herself.

The socialist in effect declares that nature is in error in having permitted diversity in respect to human-kind. It is his purpose not to permit diversity. Human beings must be compelled to be equal, he declares. They must be treated equally. Man is a collective animal. It is the good to the total mass of man that counts. It matters not what injury befalls a single man, if only the mass man benefits. Everyone is to have equal education; equal wealth; equal social status (whatever that is).

Socialism Is Not For This World

Perhaps the socialist dream can be achieved on some other planet where natural laws differ from those which function here, if such a thing is possible. It cannot be achieved here.

All nature sings the song of diversity in this world. And the individualist knows it and rejoices. He recognizes that each man is self-controlling, self-directing, responsible for his own choices and actions by virtue of the fact that he and he alone controls ALL of his own energies.

No man is ever more than one, nor ever less than one. A man may marry, have children, dedicate himself to his labors, join a hundred separate organizations, but in all of these actions his basic nature is not altered. He is still an individual. He will be born individually. He will live individually. He will die individually. Even twins are individuals. There is no such thing as a litter man, a group man, a collective man, a mass man.

Where does this illusion of collectivized man spring from? Where do fairy stories originate? Who can say what deep subliminal urging far below the surface of the conscious mind causes men to hope and pray and yearn that things will be other than they are?

But there is more to this illusion than a subliminal hope in the hearts of ignorant but idealistic people. There is a pattern here, of purpose and intent which fits the schemes and desires of the power seekers. Strabo, writing about 30 **B.C.**, says: "Poets were not alone in giving currency to myths. Long before the poets, cities and their lawgivers had sanctioned them as a useful expedient. They had some insight into the emotional nature of the rational animal. Illiterate and uneducated men, they argued, are no better than children and, like them, are fond of stories. When through descriptive narratives or other forms of representational art (politics?) they learn how terrible are divine punishments and threats, they are deterred from their evil courses. No philosopher by means of a reasoned exhortation can move a crowd of women or any random mob to reverence, piety and faith. He needs to play upon their superstition also, and this cannot be done without myths and marvels. It was, then, as bugbears to scare the simpleminded that founders of states gave their sanction to these things. This is the function of mythology and it accordingly came to have its recognized place in the ancient plan of civil society as well as in the explanations of the nature of reality."

Although Strabo does not tell us so, a myth can be employed both as a fear inducing medium to prevent evil doing, and as an inspirational medium to encourage doing good. And what more impelling myth can one devise than the myth of socialism? Think of a world in which there is no poverty; in which there is abundance for all; in which responsibility is taken by the governmental officials; and in which all people exist indulging their various whims and being guaranteed a minimum competence, simply because they happen to be human. This is a myth. There is none more impelling. How easy it is, with this kind of doctrine expounded from the hustings in democratic contests, to convince the voter that he should adhere to the political organization which promises the most for the least effort.

Deliberate Mythology

There may be an unconscious yearning for a super world in the hearts of those who succumb to socialist blandishments, but in the hearts of those who preach the doctrine there is more than a subliminal hope; there are downright crafty machinations underway with the conscious aim of seizing power and ascendancy over the masses. It is from the masses that the taxes come. And by pretending to solve the problems of the masses, the modern political pitchman can sing the song of the Lorelei and at the same time contrive to get himself on the public payroll.

No, there is more than a subconscious yearning for something for nothing. On the side of the deliberate, there is a consciously induced mythology which fosters and sustains the illusion that the world can be amended by political fiat, that nature herself will reverse her laws if only the legislature commands.

This sorry framework of distortions, misdirections and lies is deliberately set forth so that some men can and will obtain power over other men. Having discovered that the ignorant can be cozened and led, some men turn to such practices and make careers of them. And finding influence possible, they confuse influence with control. They suppose that because they can convince a certain man that the myth of socialism is a fact, they have attained control over him. And multiplying this facility so that as many as possible are affected, they imagine themselves IN CONTROL of the human race, and that they and no others are making all decisions.

Let us stick to reality. You and you alone can control your own energies. If you are urged to take a certain course, it will be your decision that sets your feet on that pathway, or it will be your decision that sets your feet in an opposite direction. No one can control your energies for you. You may be pressured, beaten, tortured, starved or even killed, but no one other than yourself can control your own energies. In the midst of torture, you may decide to change your mind and submit to the wishes of your tormentor. It is YOUR decision. Try as he will, no other human being can possibly control your energies. Only your mind will direct the muscles of your arms and legs. Only your intelligence will tell you what you are to believe.

It is true, of course, that with the use of force and violence in the hands of another you can be injured permanently and in a way that curtails your ability to control your own energies. For example, you could have an arm removed. Forever afterward you could not control that arm, since you would no longer have it. You could experience the result of lobotomy or other mental operation which might deprive you of the use of certain centers in your brain, or even your whole brain. This in no way alters the central fact. You and you alone CONTROL your own energies.

Others may, by force, succeed in atrophying your abilities. But they cannot substitute their control for yours. Even in hypnosis, it is your will to be hypnotised that makes it possible for another mind to appear to exercise control. Actually, the other mind does no such thing. Your mind is still the controlling fact, but it permits a rider. Does the equestrian control the muscles of the horse? No. The equestrian may dominate, but the horse submits and it is the will of the horse that makes submission possible. The horse's muscles still belong to the horse.

Unalienable Rights

This is what the American founding fathers were getting at when they insisted in the Declaration of Independence that man has certain unalienable rights. It was their position not only that governments may not alienate those rights, but even the men who have them cannot do it. If a right is unalienable, then the right is the same as a natural function and no one else can exercise it. Can anyone breathe for you? Can anyone operate your digestive juices for you? If you plunge your arm into a fire, can anyone else experience the pain for you? You have an unalienable right to function as nature intended that you function. And this is at the base of individualism. The natural fact of life is that you are an individual. Do what you will in connection with other people, you are still an individual, and so is each one of them. You are not primarily an American, a Chinaman, a Republican, a Democrat, a Kiwanian, a Girl Scout or a socialist. Primarily, you are individual. And even if you become a number of other things, nature insists that you always remain what you naturally are — an individual.

But, if you are naturally an individual, you cannot naturally be a collectivist, a mass man. And here is the reason why no socialist scheme has ever been retained with any degree of permanency. It is contrary to nature. Man may permit himself to be organized, regimented, dominated and coerced. This may go on for years under a Lycurgus, a Diocletian, an Inca, a Stalin or even a Roosevelt. But sooner or later, man recognizes that this condition is contrary to nature. Knowingly or unknowingly, he again aligns himself with nature. When this occurs, the forces of nature are ruthless in toppling the regimenter; civilization slides down the scale to a natural stopping point and the whole process of developing individuality, even through mistaken means, begins again. Here is the history of the world in thimble-size. It would seem that the lesson we have thus far learned from history, as B. H. Liddell Hart indicates, is that thus far we have learned nothing from history.

Individualist Origins

How can we begin to learn? Oddly enough, we have only to begin where the socialists began, in ancient times. If it is true that the Essenes and others held a universal sharing of wealth to be a moral way of life, the fact is that most men were not Essenes, and despite these teachings, whether they occurred under Buddha, Moses, Confucius or Christ, men acted out their true natures. It is as natural for a man to produce and to keep the products of his production for himself, as it is for him to breathe. Thus, for thousands of years, this is what men did. While some political overlords were contriving laws and taxes and jails for criminals, most men were going about their natural tasks of seeking to sustain life. Men, and not governments, learned how to make fire, to till the soil, to irrigate, to make bow and spear and sword, and even gunpowder. And these things were made in the ever present compulsion to find an adequate food supply, clothing, shelter, a more abundant life.

In this endless drive, some men profited more than others. But for centuries, this fact served as a double signal. It served to summon the brave, the daring, the productive, to make rugged effort, to produce, to trade, to profit in spite of all.

It is upon the efforts of such as these that civilization has advanced. It also provided the signal for the political bandits to swoop down on the successful, rob him of his surplus, and thus reduce the incentive to produce even adequately, let alone abundantly.

Since we have laid the burden of guilt at Plato's feet for first writing down the socialist dream, it is fair that we must credit another ancient Greek for having propounded the opposite of Plato's doctrines. Our reference is to Zeno (342-267 or 270 B.C.), the founder of the stoic philosophy of individualism. This sage, who came originally from Crete, opposed Plato's Republic. He repudiated the omnipotence of the state, its intervention and regimentation, and proclaimed the sovereignty of the moral law of the individual as supreme, remarking that since man was a moral being, if he were to be freed from the compulsions of the state he would respond in accordance with his true nature and have no need for courts or for police.

Unfortunately, all of Zeno's writings have been lost. We only get a fragmentary picture of this man and that is second-hand. But from what we can learn, the immortal Zeno counseled that the drive for survival would temper man's disposition in his relationship with others of his kind and cause him to become cooperative and productive, since by so becoming he would benefit himself.

It would seem that nature has endowed men to create, to invent, to produce; and at the same time that ambition has endowed governments with the socialist dogma of seeking to take from those who have, to give to those who have not. And since it is always true that no government has anything that it has not first taken from someone else, it follows that governments shall always be the first recipients of the largesse of stolen goods. So men have labored for thousands of years so that they might profit individually. And governments and a hundred dogmas have labored right alongside in an effort to prevent the diversity and the inequality which nature insists shall be the character of success and production.

So, here we have two worlds, a world of reality geared to things as they are, and a world of illusion geared to things as certain theorists wish they were. It is characteristic of man that he will trust his illusions before he will trust reality. Man is a myth maker, and a myth seeker. Man, in all his ages, is fearful of the profits some producer may amass. So he flies to the arms of the predator who gives him nothing at all except taxes, regimentation and abuse. But he does it gladly, knowing that the predator will treat the producer similarly, and that thus the producer will not be permitted to excel him.

But always, it is the world of reality that will win. Illusions come and go, but facts remain. So it is time we had a doctrine of facts on which to base our lives, rather than the many different socialist doctrines of superstition and illusion.

Christian Individualism

Curiously, we can find the beginnings of a doctrine based on natural right in the Christian religion. For if Mark advises us that Jesus intoned against the rich, and insisted that heaven was almost impossible for those who had been financially successful, Matthew tells us another story. In Chapter XXV,

14th to 30th verses, appears one of the oldest and soundest lessons in basic economics to be reduced to writing. It is the parable of the talents.

It is strangely contradictory to other statements in the four gospels, and is certainly opposed to the acts of the a-postles following the crucifixion. But without this parable it is doubtful if Christianity would have ever become a major religion. The parable provides the escape hatch for the successful and business-wise Christian. He learns here that it is not sinful to make profits; that it is prudent and, indeed, commendatory to make as much profit as possible. In the first three centuries after Christ there were few wealthy and influential men to take up the new religious doctrine. Christianity got its impetus toward material success by virtue of this idea, carefully included in the gospel of St. Matthew. Scholars are prone to believe that the parable was an addition to the original text and was appended as an afterthought. They insist that evidence abounds that the author of the book of Matthew did not pen it, for it contains characteristics of other authorship.

In any case, this is the free enterprise theory, the law of nature and of nature's way of permitting and encouraging a multiplication of goods and services. Here is the solace to the man of means, which can comfort him in the darkest hours of transitory socialist success. For this parable is purportedly recited by Jesus himself, and on it, Christianity, especially Protestant Christianity, has gone forward to seek the rewards of which the Master spoke. It has been observed that in nations predominantly Protestant, the greatest progress has been made in science, business and industrial development.

"For the Kingdom of heaven is as a man travelling into a far country, who called his own servants, and delivered unto them his goods.

"And unto one he gave five talents, to another two, and to another one; to every man according to his several ability; and straightway took his journey.

"Then he that had received the five talents went and traded with the same, and made them other five talents.

"And likewise he that had received two, he also gained other two.

"But he that had received one went and digged in the earth, and hid his lord's money.

"After a long time, the lord of those servants cometh, and reckoneth with them.

"An so he that had received five talents came and brought other five talents, saying, Lord, thou deliverest unto me five talents; behold, I have gained beside them five talents more.

"His lord said unto him, Well done, good and faithful servant: thou hast been faithful over a few things. I will make thee ruler over many things; enter thou into the joy of thy lord.

"Then he which had received the one talent came and said, Lord, I knew thee that thou art a hard man, reaping where thou has not sown, and gathering where thou has not strawed:

"And I was afraid, and went and hid thy talent in the earth; lo, there thou hast that is thine.

"His lord answered and said unto him. Thou wicked and slothful servant, thou knewest that I reap where I sowed not, and gather where I have not strawed:

"Thou oughtest therefore to have put my money to the exchangers, and then at my coming I should have received mine own with usury.

"Take therefore the talent from him, and give it unto him which hath ten talents.

"For unto every one that hath shall be given, and he shall have abundance; but from him that hath not shall be taken away even that which he hath.

"And cast ye the unprofitable servant into outer darkness: there shall be weeping and gnashing of teeth."

Here is counsel, stern and uncompromising, based upon the nature of things as they are. Here is no socialist pap, but red-blooded economic vigor. Here is praise for the man who exploits every opportunity, even perhaps an opportunity which may fall to hand accidentally. The lord in the parable harvests crops which the hand of nature alone has sowed, and he profits thereby. Here is even the recommendation that interest (usury) be collected if profits cannot be made in any other reasonable fashion. This is no precursor of Proudhon, Marx or the Fabians who with one accord thought that interest, profits and rents were wrong. Here is a sound moral source, urging production, seeing in a plentiful harvest something that will benefit all persons, especially the diligent.

Here is the opposite of Marx, who championed the concept that you should take from those with ability and give to those without ability on the basis of need. Here is, instead, the concept that those with ability should be rewarded and on the basis of that ability; whereas those without ability, even if seemingly in need, should be cast into outer darkness. This is the philosophy of something for something.

The miracle is that Mark and Matthew are believed to be reporting evidence from the same source.

In any case, here is individualism expressed economically. Nothing else of such vigor and adherence to the nature of things was to be reduced to writing until Adam Smith, in

1776, published his treatise called "The Wealth of Nations" and laid the footing for modern economic thought. There was no free enterprise Plato to decorate the age of Greece. The science of economics is of more current origin. It has taken at least twenty centuries of experimentation with shortages and socialism to convince a few that a doctrine of individualism can be logically outlined and supported as a natural and moral way of life.

CHAPTER 8

STEADY HANDS

By now it should have become apparent that there are two distinctly different types of socialism. One is voluntary in character, as exemplified by the early Christians and other groups which urged a submissive economic sharing. The other is compulsive in character, as exemplified by Marxism and the highly successful Fabian approach. Before going further, it is important that we recognize that the Fabian technique relies on violence as does the Marxian brand of compulsion.

Invisible Violence

There is a large area of thought which holds that so long as majority decisions are relied upon, no violence appears. This is a fallacy. It makes no difference to the final result whether the guns are produced visibly and employed to wrest private property from the rightful owners; or whether the guns are hidden, the appeal is made to the voters, and a majority approves of a public seizure of property or other wealth.

Force, brutal and tyrannous, is employed in both cases. If anything, the second employment of force, which withholds the guns from public gaze, is the more dangerous. It is relatively simple to arouse the public against a visible display of might. It is in the nature of human beings that they deplore violence. But it is also in the nature of human beings that they sometimes fail to recognize violence when an agency not using guns (the tax assessor) is backed up by a second agency (the sheriff) which does use the guns.

This false front of peaceful means must be recognized for what it is. Until it is recognized, great numbers of voters, enjoying what they imagine is freedom of choice, will be assembled at the polls and asked to choose between two socialist measures. Fancying that peaceful means prevail, they will, in most cases, approve the lesser socialist proposal. The approval achieved, the ranks of the socialists expand and the process of eliminating private ownership moves forward without a shot being fired.

The fulcrum on which the individual mind must pivot at this juncture is the science of economics. Who is to own what, is the key question.

Dr. F. A. Harper, in his remarkable "Liberty — A Path To Its Recovery," provides us with the clue.

"The right of a person to the product of his own labor is the foundation of economic liberty. The requirements of liberty in the economic realm can be met in no other way.

"The question at issue is how to distinguish between what is mine and what is thine. The hermit is not concerned about this matter, which becomes a problem only when two or more persons have relationships with one another.

"There are three ways to handle this problem:

"1. Each person may have whatever he can grab.

2. Some person other than the one who produces the goods and services may decide who shall have the right of possession or use.

3. Each person may be allowed to have whatever he produces.

"These three methods cover all the possibilities; there are no others."

We could point out that the attainment of freedom, economic or otherwise, is the goal of the individualist.

Let us now trace the individualistic pattern of economic thought seeing how, when it is sustained, the furtherance of human liberty is brought about.

Individualist Economics

In this tracing, our debt to Adam Smith is great. Although he erred respecting the labor theory of value, which

Ricardo and later Marx were to expand into a dogma, he correctly saw the economic picture from an individualist's point of view. He clearly stated that "by directing that industry in such a manner as its produce may be of the greatest value, he intends only his own gain.... He is in this, as in many other cases, led by an invisible hand to promote an end which was no part of his intention... By pursuing his own interest he frequently promotes that of the society more effectually than when he really intends to promote it."

In other words, the individualist, even though he is intent with his own profits, must in the market place provide for the rest of mankind. His greatest success, and hence his greatest profit, will accrue to him when he best serves others. Popular approval of his service or product must mean, if the market be free and open, that he is doing what society wants him to do. Therefore, though he gains, it follows that his gain is not made at the expense of society, but rather by society's own betterment. Under individualistic enterprise, the gain of one becomes the gain of all.

This is a dynamic philosophy which must inevitably encourage the best from all individuals. And since it can be demonstrated that the individual who profits is not depriving the rest of something it once had, but instead is providing society with something it never had before, the values of the individualistic economic format become at once apparent.

Static Economy

In contrast, the socialist philosophy is seen as nearly static. It has no encouragement for the producer. Its sole function is to divide, on as even a base as possible, everything that at one time or another has been produced.

It is not that socialists desire a static world. They are interested in an increase of wealth for everyone. They speak constantly of more production. But they prevent the creation of the wealth they desire by insisting that wealth be distributed evenly as it is created. This is contrary to the nature of things and cannot occur without the use of force.

Those who create wealth do so individually. Production occurs unevenly. There is no such thing as spontaneous general genesis of wealth. To distribute it continually by the use of force stifles its creation.

The net result of the socialist program can be reached in either of two directions: 1) a gradual diminution of wealth. 2) An increased reliance on force. The use of sufficient force to prevent the diminution of wealth would result in a static condition maintained by violence.

The socialist world will be static, it will fall apart, or it will stop being socialist.

It must follow that if division rather than multiplication is to be the mathematical formula applied to the economy, under socialism we will experience a shrinkage in all of the goods and services available. There will be no incentive to cause the individual to produce all he can. Consequently, society will be injured by his failure to seek as great a profit as possible. In fact — and the matter is one of common knowledge gleaned from observation of the many controlled societies that have had existence, as well as from observation of those societies which have been relatively uncontrolled — superior individuals, instead of seeking to make as much profit as they can, and thereby to enrich society, will produce only as much as they can produce with a minimum of predation against them.

The man capable of $100,000 worth of production in a given year who finds that $90,000 worth will be taken from him, is constrained to produce only $10,000 worth. Society thus loses the benefit of the $90,000 worth which remains un-produced. And even though the $10,000 worth of production is equally divided, it follows that society is harmed for it cannot benefit by sharing in something that has not been produced.

Carlyle saw the implications of the Adam Smith analysis and dubbed it "anarchy plus a constable." He was not refer-ring to the anarchy of Proudhon or Bakunin, but only to the theoretical anarchy which would follow the elimination of all government interventionism in the economic structure.

In short, the individualist economic position has been scurrilously attacked by socialists on the grounds that it tends to create an unbalanced society. The fact is the individualist economic position tends to improve society and is a better and more natural balancing procedure than the static philosophy of share-the-wealth, however unbalanced an economy may become.

There can be no sale without a purchase. Whatever goods are sold, must also be bought. And if there is no intervention in the economic laws of supply and demand, society will freely purchase that which it wants from the stocks of those things which have been produced. Thus, the individualist economic idea, generally termed **"laissez-faire"** (let it alone), ought to be more acceptable to socialists than the socialist doctrine. Since the aim of the socialist is allegedly the good of all society, and since it can be demonstrated that the good of all society is achieved best by freedom for the individual members of society to produce in an unlimited and unhampered manner, relying on societal acceptance, the real aim of the individualist, to make a profit, enhances the societal aim of the socialist.

We must, at this point, either accuse the socialist of bad faith or of intellectual ineptitude. Either accusation could be authenticated in specific cases. The dread of the socialist is centered in inequality; he cannot, or will not recognize the natural laws of humankind which make it impossible for two people to be identical. He insists that at whatever cost, this static sameness be achieved. He abandons his idealistic end — the good of all society — and becomes lost in a sea of means which are fundamentally immoral. But so fervently is this sophistry believed, that it becomes tantamount to heresy to point out the error. In fact, equality becomes the single moral absolute.

Each Is Unique

But equality, so far as the genus **homo sapiens** is concerned, is more of a political shibboleth than anything else. From a psychological standpoint, each individual human being is unique. And now we have the remarkable study by Professor Roger J. Williams of the University of Texas, to assure us that physical individuality is no less a fact than psychological variance. He says:

"My own particular interest in this subject probably stems from the laboratory observation, over twenty years ago, that, although creatine was described by Beilstein as a bitter biting substance, it was found to be absolutely tasteless to many. About the same time, I noted that some otherwise normal individuals were unable to detect skunk odor. I began to be convinced more than ten years ago that DIFFERENCES between human beings (as well as their similarities) needed to be brought to light, because they are crucially important factors which must be taken into account if many human problems are to be solved. The ideas which grew out of this concept were set forth in two books, 'The Human Frontier' and 'Free and Unequal.' When my interest in this area first developed I regarded it as considerably divergent from my chosen field of research — biochemistry. However, as time has gone on and research results have accumulated, it has become clearer to me that individuality and applied biochemistry are inextricably intertwined. I no longer regard my interest in individuality as a departure from biochemistry." ("Biochemical Individuality," John Wiley & Sons, Inc.).

We are beginning to learn that each man is unique not only insofar as his political and economic predilections are concerned, but from the standpoint of biology, biochemistry, chemistry and even organic structure. The more we learn, the more futile appears to be the socialist dogma of "sameness," "togetherness," "conformity," and "universal division of wealth."

Now let us review the individualist economic position briefly. It begins with the admission that while all humankind are unequal, all humankind have certain basic and unalienable rights which they hold in common, and in these rights have a brotherhood, if not an equality.

Be it noted that the individualist does not concern himself with the perplexing problem of morality among cows, chickens, trees, grasses and insects. He is concerned with establishing a moral base for mankind. The individualist wishes to see this planet as one on which life is pleasant and productive for his own kind. He may be tenderhearted respecting other forms of life and a conservationist at heart respecting trees and flowers. But respecting these other forms of life he is not a Jain, moving about with broom to brush each beetle out of his pathway lest he inadvertently crush one to death.

Two Types of Energy

He begins by recognizing that there are two types of energy operating on this planet, and two types only. One he classes as human energy; the other, as non-human energy. His concern is with human energy. He does not wish to see it wasted, misdirected or destroyed. As to non-human energy, this must be harnessed so that it serves humankind, or it must be reduced at least to neutrality so that it does not injure or destroy humankind. Life on this planet is no idyllic passage of time in a sort of everlasting Eden. Man wars endlessly against insects, disease, drought, excesses in temperature, the ravages of wild beasts, exposure and starvation. Each advance in the uses of human energy is an improvement for all human energies. Each retreat before some onslaught of non-human energies poses a threat to the entire species.

Realistically, the individualist holds that it is not a moral breach if he smashes a beetle. He will raise cattle for food, harness horses for power, stalk deer in the wilderness and do whatever else is needful, including the felling of trees and the harnessing of rivers, so that humankind may benefit.

And here the individualist states that there are certain self-evident truths which, while they may not be susceptible of proof, nonetheless are valid beginnings for his argument. He holds that all men have certain rights; that these rights are universally applicable. He also holds that a right is not a privilege. A privilege is a special permission which is granted by certain persons with power, to other persons, and is not inherent, nor is it universally applicable. The true individualist wishes to see an end to privilege and an acceptance of universal rights.

Again we must give credit to Dr. F. A. Harper for the following. These are not the professor's words, but are the essence of a lecture delivered at the Freedom School in 1957.

Five Steps

The first right held by all men is the right to live. It is essential that we begin here. And it follows that if every man has a right to live, no man has a right to interfere with that right in another. Clearly, this is moral ground. Equally clear is the fact that if we accept this basic postulate, man must not prey on other men, but must instead employ his energies against the non-human agencies in nature for his existence. He may not kill another man. He may do as he pleases respecting non-man. He cannot thwart nature. But he can combat its destructive tendencies and harness its constructive usages.

The second right which follows the first, is that all men have a right to sustain their lives. The first cannot be true without the second. Therefore, man is a warrior, combatant in the natural arena, wresting his living from all areas except those occupied by other men.

And now the third: If man has a right to sustain his own life, clearly he has a right to produce whatever he wishes to produce, so that his living can be sustained. This world is not a paradise. Man does not lie under a bread-fruit tree and have his sustenance drop into his mouth without effort. Man must convert the products of nature for his own use. Houses must be built, clothes must be manufactured, food must be grown and harvested. These things do not occur naturally. They occur only when man harnesses his energy and produces the things he needs and wants. If a man has a right to sustain his life, he must have a right to produce. Maintenance of life is impossible otherwise.

The fourth right is in logical progression from the original right. If man has a right to produce, then he must have a right to use what he produces in his own best interests. This means that he must have the right to consume or to save the products of his own energy. It follows, then, that man has a right to own, to possess. And those things which are his, are his absolutely. If one man produces much and another little, the basic right is unaffected. Each man has a right to the totality of his production. No other man has any right to any part of the production of another.

But now we see the inevitable conclusion. If man has a right to use whatever he has in any way he sees fit, then he has a right to save, to invest, to buy, to sell, to give away, or even to destroy wantonly that which is his. And if this is true, then man has a right to individual ownership. More, he has a right to be a capitalist. For a capitalist is simply the person who saves what he produces today and invests it so that there can be more production tomorrow. Thus, capitalism becomes not only a sound economic procedure, and politically should be sacrosanct, it is at once a moral position. The owner, manipulator and controller of non-human energies is essentially a moral man. Those men who devote themselves in an effort to control other men, or to wrest from them those non-human energies they have acquired, must be essentially immoral.

If a man has a right to life, then he has a right to own property privately. If he has a right to own property privately, he has a right to be a capitalist.

Let us approach the individualist position respecting economics in another way. Economics has been variously described and defined. Let us simply conclude that it deals with man's material well-being, and that it is a science which sets forth the kind of human action necessary to create and enlarge upon that well-being.

Basic Equation

The primary essentials to man's material well-being are: natural resources, human energy and tools. That is all there is. We are aided by the quotation furnished by the American Economic Foundation and its two analysts, Mr. Fred G. Clark and Mr. Richard S. Rimanoczy: $MMW = NR + HE \times T$.

We see here that man's material well-being is equal to natural resources, plus human energy, multiplied by tools.

This means that everything in the world that human beings want and can use is the product of these three things. A moment's reflection is all that is necessary to apprise ourselves of these facts. The whole world is full of natural resources. These are the minerals, metals, plants, animals, soils, waters and all the natural products of the earth. Man does not provide those things. They are provided by nature; hence, we call them natural resources. Certain things we may not recognize at a given moment as being resources.

To begin with, when the early settlers moved West across the vast stretches of American prairie and forest, the natural resource that first appealed was the wild life. Animals were hunted for food and for clothing. Other resources were overlooked. Later, other men came seeking a use for timber, or they sought to clear land so that is could be planted to food crops. Still later, men sought for minerals and oils and metals.

In the West right now, the shift in emphasis on natural resources is evident. A hundred years ago, gold was the magnet that drew men into the hills. There were many other kinds of ores available, but gold was what was wanted. For awhile men were seeking frantically for a kind of ore called uranium. It was always there in the hills, just as the gold had been, but men did not know its uses. Now that science has opened the doors of atomics and electronics, uranium can be even more important than gold. And who knows what new uses may be found in time for the most commonplace items that nature has provided?

The problem that has always confronted men in respect to natural resources is this: How do you get at the resources? Crops do not plant themselves, cultivate themselves, harvest and store themselves. Metals do not leap from the earth; they must be mined, smelted, refined, and processed before they can be used. Trees do not fell themselves; they must be cut, trimmed, hauled, milled, and then retailed through thousands of outlets. Everywhere men are busy upon the face of the earth now, attacking the mountains of natural resources and converting them to use.

So, for men to have material well-being, natural resources are useless and valueless until human energy has been applied.

Tools Are The Crux

And now we come to the crux of the matter. For man, that strange and illogical biped, grows arms and legs instead

of tools. Primitive man learned how to use primitive tools —
stone axes, hammers, spears. Until he had his first crude tool
he was no better than a beast. As time passed, he began to
improve his tools. The better and more useful his tools became, the more readily did the natural resources succumb to
his attack. A man with his bare hands cannot mine coal. Give
him a spade and he can begin to work. But it would take
thousands of man-hours using spades to provide even the beginnings of a modern coal mine.

So the tools have been improved. Now we have great
electric or diesel shovels, electric drills, air pressure drills,
lifts, ventilators, cable cars and even automatic scoops, con-
veyor belts, railroad cars and a thousand other things from
the tiniest wrench to the big diesel engines, all of which are
used to mine coal. The result of the improvement in the use
of tools is that more coal can be mined in a shorter space of
time so that more people in society can have the benefits that
a use of coal can bring to them. Further, by the development
of mass means of both mining and manufacture, prices have

dropped. The advantage again accrues to society which is now able to purchase more for a smaller investment of its own time and energy.

It is not our purpose here to provide all the economic arguments. What we are trying to show is the superiority of individualistic efforts over socialistic efforts. And under an individualistic economy, there is major incentive to save money so that it can be invested. This is true because investments provide a second way any human being can earn. He can earn through his own labors; and he can earn additionally by saving something of what he earns, investing it somewhere in the production and development of tools, and then he can receive interest or dividends on his money thus invested. All tools are the result of individual initiative and effort. All tools are paid for out of savings. And in an individualistic economy both forms of earnings are always available to anyone who will individually make the requisite effort and sacrifice.

Thus, while the socialist cries for equality and endeavors to use the force of guns and law to provide it, the individualist recognizes a natural equality of opportunity, and according to his own wisdom and his own conscience does what he believes is best for himself. In the process he cannot prevent being helpful to society. Thus, in fact, and according to the nature of things, there is greater real equality to be found in an individualistic economy than can be found in a socialist economy.

In an individualistic economy, each person may do all he can, and is free to profit without limit according to his own ability to provide what the rest of society is willing to pay for. In a socialist economy, each person may do only those things he is permitted to do by the gracious permission of a central authority. He cannot make profit. Nor can he provide profit for society. He can only serve within the limits prescribed.

The result of the individualistic economy is all about us in America. Only here in all the world and in all of time, has there been enough of an individualistic economy to provide abundance. Elsewhere, under various degrees of socialistic control, shortages and scarcity are the rule.

There are so many advantages to private individualistic ownership, and so few to public and collectivized ownership, that the argument is top-heavy in favor of freedom and private ownership at the outset. Yet, despite the evidence, the movement toward world socialism continues.

There must be a reason so many continue to support socialism by their words and their deeds. It cannot be written off as a case of simple subversion in which a minority of enemy agents seize control and exercise dominion. Nor can it be written off as a matter of moral zeal. Against the moral position of the socialists — that all men must share equally — is the moral position of the individualist — that no man has a right to steal.

Roots of the Problem

The problem must go deeper. There may be a number of reasons for the ascendancy of the socialist philosophy in the twentieth century. But let us submit that there is one, all-encompassing reason. It is this. People still do not understand the true nature of socialism, particularly when it is advanced by people they know and trust. They have not learned to recognize socialism's true character. If this is correct, then the reason we have such a tendency to advance into socialism is because the very persons who presume themselves to be opposed to socialism, in fact are not opposed. There may be some particular part of socialism that they abhor. But they do oppose it only in specific cases.

Let us sum up, then, the all-encompassing reason for continued promotion of the socialist myth. One word covers it: Ignorance. And the answer to ignorance, now and always, is education. Enlightenment. We are not referring to the government institutions of indoctrination which presently serve as public schools and which concentrate on convincing our youth that capitalism and free enterprise are "outmoded," "passe," and "18th century thinking." We are referring to true enlightenment, which is based upon the reality of man's existence on this planet.

Many doctors oppose socialized medicine, for example. But they do not oppose socialized housing, socialized farming, socialized libraries, socialized welfare in other areas than medicine. These doctors will parade as being strongly anti-socialist. Actually, they are full-fledged socialists in many areas save medicine.

Many a contractor is opposed to socialized housing. But the contractor will favor socialized medicine, socialized security, socialized golf courses, socialized aviation, and even socialized loans for buyers of homes. These contractors appear to be anti-socialists. Actually, they are in the vanguard of those helping to turn this nation and the world into a polyglot socialist state.

It does little good to oppose socialism in one area while welcoming it with open arms in other areas. The anti-socialist conviction is cancelled out by a flood of pro-socialism.

So it is time for us to examine socialism further in an effort to isolate the germ. Let us bear in mind that now we

are concerning ourselves with destructive and harmful socialism. The unworldly and innocuous brand of share-the-
wealth on a voluntary basis is no longer under our purview.

CHAPTER 9

ONE MAN'S BREAD

We must return to Adam Smith.

This great economist and father of the modern theory of free markets propounded an error which has haunted us ever since.

Smith's "labor theory of value" was mistaken. However, Ricardo accepted it and elaborated it. As elaborated by Ricardo, the labor theory of value was still further developed by Marx. Thus, we have a socialist theory of economic value resultant from a doubly compounded error. This error has become the moral fulcrum on which the political socialist lever rests.

What Smith was getting at, and what most individualists would agree with, is the moral certainty that the laborer is entitled to the full product of his own labor. Indeed, earlier in this essay that has been listed as a basic right of every human being.

Getting All That You Earn

The "surplus value" theory of Marx is derived from the "labor theory of value" of Smith and Ricardo. Briefly, the theory can be explained thusly: It is evident that natural resources do not prepare themselves for the use of man. Human energy and tools must be applied to the resources before they can be converted into usable form and transported to places where a demand for them exists.

One does not pay money to natural resources. Nor does one pay money to tools. It may be an essential to pay the person who owns the resources or the tools. But essentially, all money passes from one human hand into another human hand. And the passage relates to the amount of labor performed by the human energy supplied in each case.

Thus, one does not buy logs or lumber for building; one purchases the labor that has gone into the felling of the trees, the milling of the lumber. What are the logs worth while they are still trees? Fundamentally, they are worth whatever it costs to convert them. And here is Marx: If more than that basic cost of labor is included in the purchase price, the element of profit or "surplus value" appears. If you must pay a lumberman $5.00 to fell a tree, trim it, saw it into usable lengths and thicknesses, and then deliver it, the tree is worth $5.00, no more, no less.

Superficially, this is reasonable enough — reasonable, that is, if this were a world in which hand tools were all that could ever be employed, land could never be privately owned, and our wants were such simple things as log houses. We are far from such a world; such a world is contrary to the nature of man's basic rights; there is no desire for such a world. The "labor theory of value" is fallacious and the notion of "surplus value" based upon it is equally in error.

What Smith, Ricardo and Marx have done and what the followers of the latter two continue to do, is to confuse the meanings of two important words: cost and value. While it may be true in the above instance that it might cost $5.00 to produce the lumber from a given tree, the value of the lumber from that tree has no immediate relationship to cost.

Value, as Bohm-Bawerk, Ludwig von Mises and others demonstrate is inevitably the result of a subjective judgment. Lumber may cost $5.00, but the intensity with which you, as a purchaser, desire the lumber determines whether it is worth $1.00 or $20.00 to you. If it is worth only $1.00 to you, you will not purchase it if it is priced above that sum, regardless of the cost expended in producing it. Similarly, if you would be glad to pay as much as $20.00 for it, you will consider it a bargain if it is priced at $10.00, even though the cost of producing the lumber was $5.00 and the other $5.00 represents a profit to the producer.

In short, as a purchaser, you do not consider either cost or profit to others. You concern yourself with value, which relates to your own desire and your own ability to pay.

It is in this area that Smith, et al, come to grief. They conclude that cost and value are the same thing.

Two Kinds of Pies

Perhaps an illustration will best provide the demonstration. We are indebted to Leonard E. Read of the Foundation of Economic Education for the illustration. Let us suppose that "A" has a bakery. He hires a number of workers, buys the best raw materials, and produces the finest mince pies in town. His costs, including the interest on the money he has borrowed, the rent of the land he uses, and all of the other factors that enter into the equation, make it possible for him to produce these pies and deliver them to your door for 40¢.

He charges 50¢.

Marx would insist that he should sell at a figure which excludes interest. But he may pay himself a salary for his pains. Marx in "Das Kapital" recognizes the validity of managerial work, contrary to popular belief, and wishes it to be paid for at a modicum. Marx will not recognize a profit as a legitimate part of the economic cycle. So in the above case, he would hold that the man who has run the risk, borrowed the money, bears the responsibility, manages the enterprise and owns the tools, should receive only a salary and no more. We will deal with this idea in a moment. Let us concentrate on the 50¢ mince pie. At this price, the owner and manager can pay himself a salary and in addition can accrue a profit if business is brisk.

Now, let us consider "B." "B" also has a bakery. He hires the same number of workers as "A," buys the best raw materials, and produces the finest mud pies in town. His costs, the interest on the money he has borrowed, the rent of the land he uses, and all of the other factors that enter into the equation make it possible for him to produce these mud pies and deliver them to your door for exactly the same price as the mince pies of his competitor, "A." Now whether "B" insists on a profit or not, the fact of the matter is that it is almost inconceivable to imagine a going business in mud pies.

But, if Smith, Ricardo and Marx are correct, then the product of "A's" factory which costs 40¢ to produce must be valued at precisely the value of the product of "B's" factory, since this product, also, costs just 40¢ to produce. If value is determined by cost, the mud pies and mince pies are of equal value if the sum expended to produce is equal.

Certainly, this is ridiculous. But this is the labor theory of value, to wit: The cost of the human energy expended in the production of any commodity, is the value of the commodity.

One has only to imagine a situation such as this: Some enterprising genius discovers a way to manufacture yachts by an extrusion process which makes the cost of a yacht so small that it can be purchased in quantity lots for as little as $100 each. A second individual discovers a way to make elaborate igloos of ice and snow, completely equipped with air conditioning, which cost $1,000 each because of all the hand labor which must be utilized in the construction. In the Marxian catalogue, the igloo would be worth ten times what the yacht would be worth, regardless of the fact that many people would like to buy the yacht and there are virtually no takers for the igloos.

But, under Marxian or Fabian socialism, both industries would be owned and operated by the government, the taxpayers would underwrite the costs of both, and thus all persons would help to pay for igloos, of which few, if any, are wanted.

It is inconceivable that rational human beings could endorse such stupidity, but so cleverly have the results of socialist fallacy been hidden from them, and so thoroughly are they imbued with the holy grail of equality, that they shut their eyes to the certain results and blindly support the doctrine.

Question of Profit

Now let us examine more closely the "surplus value" concept, since the "labor theory of value" has been revealed for what it is. What Marx and other socialists envisage is the elimination of all profits, interest and rent. What we must immediately do is to examine the nature of enterprise to discover, if we can, if enterprise can exist without the socalled element of "surplus value," or profit.

Here the socialists contribute to their own downfall. For virtually, without exception, the socialist wishes to see all costs of production paid. What he is getting at, he says, is not the cheating of any human being, but rather the elimination of cheating. He wants the laborer to be paid what he is worth and not one cent less.

Very well, what are the costs of doing business? Again, we are indebted to the American Economic Foundation. There are only five costs. Whatever business you wish to select as an illustration, five costs will cover all expenses in connection with its operation. These five costs are:

1. Goods and services furnished by others.

NB The socialist will have no objection to meeting this payment. He expects those who furnish services and goods to be reimbursed. He just wants to make certain that profits are eliminated. But he has no objection to a person paying for the goods or services he hires. In fact, the socialist would insist that these things be paid for.

2. Human energy.

NB Here the socialist will wax eloquent. This is precisely the point, he will tell you. He wants the human energy paid for at full cost value. So he certainly has no objection to Item 2.

3. Taxes.

NB Here again you will find no objection from the dyed-in-the-wool-wealth-sharer. Since he is probably privy to the fact that the socialist movement is in the process of transferring all goods and all wealth out of private hands and into the hands of the state, the socialist will strongly support taxes, even high taxes, which others must pay.

4. Maintaining tools.

NB This one will cause the socialist to review his position slightly. But if one presents his facts carefully, one can usually convince the collectivist that machines do wear out and must be replaced. Further, machines can be improved upon and such improvements or replacements cost money. After careful review, the socialist will concede, though begrudgingly, for he rarely thinks about such mundane things as repairs, research and maintenance, that Item 4 is an essential. If tools aren't replaced they are broken or worn out and there will be no more work. There is no job in existence which does not require a certain amount of tooling, from the steel man with his enormous blast furnaces, to the door-to-door salesman selling brushes.

5. Using the tools.

NB Again we remind the socialist that tools do not grow on trees, nor do they protrude from the wrist of **homo sapiens**. Tools have to be made. Also, they have to be paid for. And somewhere the money has to be found to provide the tools of production. If you can convey the idea of paying for the use of tools as well as the purchase of goods and services, the socialist is defeated. This is the most difficult point to get across. But non-socialists will ultimately see that the man who owns the tools will not permit others to use them unless he is paid for so doing. Why should he? Why should anyone share what he has with someone else unless he gets something in return? So the tool owner wants to be paid for his goods and services, just as the shopkeeper wishes to be paid for his goods and the worker wishes to be paid for his labor. If you will not pay for the goods, you are not entitled to them. If you will not pay for the labor, you are not entitled to it. If you will not pay for the use of the tools, you are not entitled to use them.

If this is finally granted, behold, we have covered the item of profit. Profit is the payment to the owner of the tool for its use. The owner of the tool can be anyone. Tools can be owned by individuals, partnerships or corporations. In the latter case, and especially when large and expensive tools are required, stockholders are the true owners. But whether the owner uses the tool himself or permits others to use it, a payment for that use is both essential and honest.

We have by no means exhausted this subject. But if a little time is spent on this formula of the five costs of production, it is simple to establish that there is no such thing as "surplus value," and that the "labor theory of value" is an oversimplification.

CHAPTER 10

THE GREATEST MYTH

Let us again consider the political format of socialism. Socialism — which is at its roots a system of sharing the wealth and therefore is an economic theory — when combined with a political instrument becomes a device for compulsory redistribution of wealth. It is the word COMPULSORY which must now come under examination.

The modern socialist, beginning about the time of Godwin, was no longer content to dream of the day when life could be transformed to meet equalitarian wishes. Since for hundreds of years the dream of socialism had been advocated philosophically and religiously, without noticeable results, something more immediate and drastic was deemed essential to twist creation into a new shape more consonant with universality and equality. The government was called into play to provide the compulsion hitherto lacking.

Not by Association of Persons

We have already reviewed Marx and the Fabians as to the methods advocated since 1842. What we must do is to plunge more deeply into the definition so that we can recognize the harmful (compulsive) brand of socialism without recourse to the use of names and the device of discovering the malady by the association of persons.

It may be a shortcut to the discovery of socialist spheres of influence to be able to prove that Marx was a socialist, that Jones teaches Marxism and that Smith, who attended Jones' class, must therefore be a Marxist. The difficulty here is that the assumption is a non-sequitur. Smith may have attended Jones' classes, but may have done so in order to understand what he completely opposes. And, likewise, Jones, despite the fact that he may teach Marxism, may do so in an honest and sincere manner which falls short of either propaganda or endorsement. What is essential is the isolation of the germ itself, regardless of the names of the persons who carry it. This is mandatory if individualism is to survive.

There are two phases to compulsive socialism. These two phases have been set forth most succinctly by Marx, who said: "From each according to his ability; to each according to his need." Clearly, phase one deals with the taking according to ability; phase two, with the granting according to need. Thus, socialism begins with forceful extraction of wealth from those who have wealth, and the cycle is completed when the wealth is redistributed and finds its way into the hands of others who apparently are in need.

In phase one there are several indices which may be helpful to characterize a particular program as being socialist in nature. For example, the taking is supposed to involve those who have. Also, since we are now concerned with compulsive taking, there must be an act of force in which the taking is brought about. This means that an unnamed party must exist in the equation to bring off the theft. Certainly, there would be few with "ability" who would voluntarily part with what they have. The unnamed party is inevitably the government or some agency which is endowed with or usurps the functions of government.

Therefore, a certain guide to this phase of socialism is the intrusion of the government or a similarly endowed agency which proposes to take from those who have "ability." As to a discovery of socialism by deciding who has ability, the route is clouded with obstacles. Everyone has ability of one sort or another. And since the taking does not have to be in money, but can consist of goods, services or even in a loss of efficiency under harassment, it is difficult, if not impossible, to characterize a program as socialistic simply on the basis of the temporary financial ratings of those from whom something is being taken. As a matter of fact, a sales tax, which is assessed against any item of merchandise which changes hands, could be a tax levied principally against persons of small means, yet it could still be a device to redistribute wealth.

This is especially true when such programs as government unemployment insurance, social security and old age benefits are part of a wide front of redistribution. Those employed, regardless of the size of their wages, are inevitably better off than those unemployed. Hence, the worker earning even as little as $100 per year is better off than an unemployed person. Consequently, to take something from the employed worker is to take from one who has ability greater than the ability shown by the non-worker.

Consider, too, government programs which promote health, education and welfare. Obviously, it is consonant with socialism for those having health to share something with those who are less healthy, even if the sharing is translated into a tax program, and expressed in terms of money. Those without education become beneficiaries under socialism. And those lacking in anything else, whatever it may be, will always find themselves a little lower on the economic ladder in relation to this lack than those who may have other lacks in other fields.

Thus, in some respects, each of us is superior to someone else, and in that respect the target of the socialist leveler. It is not too harsh to say that all programs adopted by any government which tax special groups, which tax on a graduated scale, or which tax universally, are in the process of taking wealth from those with ability. In recent days in these United States, the mere ability to pay a tax, however outrageous or unjust it might be, is virtually a signal for the tax to be levied and collected. Ability to pay is considered the major key. But ability to pay ties directly into the Marxian theme and can unquestionably be traced to socialist thinking.

Socialist Giving

Let us return to this matter of **taking** a little later and consider new the matter of **giving** to those who are in need.

Once more we note a pair of clues which will help us discover socialism in action. The first is that what is to be given is to go to those who are in need. The second is that the giving is to be accomplished by an unnamed third party which is able to determine the extent and the urgency of the need. Once more, the government is indicated in this second case. Only a government could pretend to such universal omnipotence as to undertake such an impossible feat.

But, as in the prior case, we will have difficulty in discovering just who are those in need. Just as every human being has some ability, so every human being is in need. Abilities and needs do not appear to be in balance in the individual for regardless of the financial condition of the individual, his needs will far outrun his abilities. All of us want more than we have, whether we are paupers or millionaires. So once again we are baffled if we attempt to trace the socialist germ simply by assuming that only when a government gives money to the poor, is socialism operative.

An example of the corollary of this is found readily in the farm subsidy program. By far and away the largest checks in the government's soil conservation program are being handed to large and prosperous firms and agricultural operators.

Few would deny the socialistic implications. Clearly, in this case the government is sharing the taxes it has collected from hordes of small wage earners with large and wealthy land owners and operators.

Socialism is not simply a process of taking from the rich and giving to the poor. It is a process of taking from those with ability (everyone) and redistributing on some basis which is politically advantageous to those in need (everyone).

It may be argued that the government gives only to the poor. But we have disproved that above by showing, for example, the farm soil bank program in operation which rewards persons of wealth.

It may also be argued that those who are poor, who do receive from the government, are not making a contribution for their own government dole. But this can readily be disproved if we understand the enormous variations in the government's program of collecting taxes. All of us are consumers. We cannot stay alive without eating food, wearing clothing and living in some kind of shelter. There is no longer such a thing as untaxed food, untaxed clothing, or untaxed shelter. And those who consume these goods or use these services are paying taxes, even if all the money they employ in the process consists of governmental largesse. Thus, even the poorest of us is paying for our subsidy in whole or in part. And if it is only in part, the excess which we receive via the government, over and above our own contributions through taxes, is more than offset by the reduction in productive energy which is meanwhile being experienced by all others who are directly making up the difference. There is no such thing as something for nothing. All of us pay for what we get, either directly or indirectly, by the loss in productive energy of others which might otherwise provide services or products at lower prices from which each of us could benefit.

There are two factors here which require comment. It should be noted that for this unwanted and unnecessary (to all but socialists) service, the government collects and keeps an enormous brokerage fee. Thus, in the process of taking from some to give to others, the net result is a diminution of the original wealth which is held in private hands. Here, the prime objective of socialism is served. It is the aim of the socialist, you will recall, to eliminate private ownership. Any sum of money, any kind of property, which is taken from some under any excuse whatsoever and which remains in government hands, furthers the socialist goal. And when sufficient of wealth and property has been taken from the private and original owners so that control of the uses of that wealth and property is transferred to the government, even though title remains in the possession of the rightful owners, then the socialist aim is achieved.

Socialist Taking

The second point to which our attention should be directed is this. Most persons are so entranced with the idea of the giving phase of socialism that they fail to recognize a socialist coup in the taking stages. This makes socialism inordinately difficult to recognize until the transaction is completed. Many people recognize that socialism is the redistribution of wealth. What most seem unable to recognize is that no redistribution can occur until the prior collection has been completed. Thus, even well-informed individualists are placed at a tremendous disadvantage. They inveigh heartily against the sharing of wealth which almost all persons enjoy if they happen to be classed with a needy group at a given moment, but they are mute and tongue-tied at the mass theft which precedes any such sharing and which no one enjoys when he happens to be a part of the mass that is being plundered.

We think of socialism as a "share-the-wealth" scheme. We should begin to recognize it as a "take-the-wealth" scheme.

So the anti-socialist individual wears the mantle of the man who is trying to do away with Santa Claus. And the socialist wears the mantle of the one who is seeking to provide untold benefits to humanity. The opposite is the truth. The individual who wishes to preserve the rights of everyone to his own property is seeking to bestow untold benefits, and the socialist who is trying to plunder the world is the man who is in the process of destroying the overflowing cornucopia provided by a free market.

So in the result to be experienced, the individualist is always working from the tail end of the tragedy, trying to regain ground that has been lost. He is inevitably on the defensive so long as he does not oppose the plundering until it has been done. Then, he enters the arena as an opponent of the popular distribution. He comes too late to oppose the unpopular predation.

Keeping in mind the **taking** phase of socialism, there is a very serious widespread misunderstanding respecting government's role in the operation. This misunderstanding produces two fallacies. One is that a democratic form of government is a safeguard against socialism. The other, more prevalent elsewhere than in these United States, is that a strong man — an aristocrat, an autocrat or a monarch — can defeat socialism. Both of these ideas are false. Socialism, compulsive and harmful, is aided and abetted by ANY KIND of government.

If it is remembered that socialism is an economic theory respecting a sharing of wealth, and that it is made possible by governmental interference in the economy, the misunderstanding should be dispelled. It makes no difference whether the government has the form of a dictatorship, an oligarchy, a democracy, a republic, a theocracy, a monarchy, a plutocracy, or any possible combination of these or other forms. When a government taxes some for the benefit of all; when it taxes all for the benefit of some; when it attempts to provide something that the people "need," socialism is inherent.

So it must be asked if it is possible to have a government which is non-socialistic in character. And the answer is that it is not possible.

All governments tend to move toward socialism. The larger and more vigorous they become, the more surely are they practicing socialism.

This is undoubtedly the most difficult point for many to grasp. Let us explore this idea in the ensuing pages. And let us also recall that whereas all governments in all of history have practiced socialism to some degree, it remained for the advent of the 19th and 20th centuries before governmental policy consciously and deliberately espoused the socialist cause.

CHAPTER 11

PLAN OF ESCAPE

Our problem in understanding government begins when we seek to understand the word itself. In earlier pages, it has been pointed out that only the individual controls himself. It is possible for one individual to influence another; to injure another; to dominate another. It is not possible for one individual to control another. The motor nerves that control the muscles, the mysterious processes of thought and motivation are centered in each individual's mind and are unalienable.

Control of the individual resides in the individual. Anything that appears otherwise is a hoax or an illusion.

But government, by its very derivation, presumes such control. To govern, means to control others. That such control is contrary to nature, is generally not recognized. Humankind has accepted the idea of such control as a fact for thousands of years. Men have acted in their comings and goings as though they were controlled, just as pre-Renaissance man acted as though the world were flat. The fact that men believe that governments can control them does not make it so.

Superstition

What we are dealing with here is a superstition older than history. So deeply imbedded in the mores of the species is this fallacy, that it is almost impossible for modern man to permit in his consciousness the revolutionary thought that only he controls himself. To suggest it as a possible fact can induce a state of near shock. To argue it as a demonstrable fact is tantamount to causing a state of mental paralysis.

Nonetheless, the fact can be demonstrated. The single thing on which all governments base their existence is the belief in the mind of man that he can be and indeed is governed and controlled by this instrumentality. Were this belief to perish, political forms would become as archaic and useless as the second brain at the posterior of the stegosaurus. Amid the crashing of toppling governments, man would emerge properly identified as what he is, an individual, not a mass man. The consternation in the ranks of the collectivists at this statement will require no embroidery. There is enough of the collectivist in virtually every reader to send his mind whirling into outer-space by this assertion.

Thus, government is at once both a hoax and an illusion. It cannot do what it is designed to do. If it appears to accomplish some of the things it is called on to perform, its accomplishment must be credited to man's blind and ritualistic acceptance of robotism under false persuasion.

But we must begin where we are. Man believes that governments control him. Therefore, he acts as though this were true. So in the use of the word, government, it will be employed to mean the kind of supposed control exercised by some over others, contrary to the true nature of mankind.

What is the true function of government? This question has never been satisfactorily answered in any age. The answer has shifted all the way from the supposition that the ruler was a divine emissary from God's throne and as such was to make all decisions for all men, to an institution set up by men for the purpose of protecting the freedom of those who set it up. Either assumption is faulty, and all possible gradations between these two extremes fall short of the mark.

The truth is, governments are established because of the general conviction on the part of the human race that man must not be permitted to be an individual, but rather must be compelled to act out a type of "togetherness" with all other men within a specified geographical area. And since this idea has led to enormous bloodshed and perpetual war, we now have the extension of the idea to its logical conclusion, namely, that geographic limits must be abolished and all men, wherever located, must be compelled to react to a single set of controls manipulated by a single super government. This is the crowning folly. It is the extension of the socialist idea to the socialist ultimate — until such time as man bridges the gap between the planets and seeks to establish a universal government of a solar system.

Jungle Background

The idea is a carryover from our jungle years. Man begins in primitive surroundings as a congenital collectivist. He may have no formal institution of "government" as we ordinarily employ the word. But he is dominated at each moment by taboos, by tribal consciousness which causes him to think of himself more as an integral part of a whole than as a self-conscious, self-responsible individual. Aboriginal languages have no word for "I." Primitive peoples do not understand or think in terms of personality. To them, the tribe is the human being.

Voluntary individual action is the beginning of civilization. It creates civilization and civilization itself breeds further desire and necessity for voluntary individual action. The one aids and abets the other.

A useful illustration comes to mind. All primitive peoples, believing as they did in socialism, or in tribal and group values, imagined God to exist in similar societal or tribal fashion. All ancient religions depicted a chief god with a pantheon of lesser gods and goddesses. Heaven and earth were but a mirrored reflection of each other. The chief on earth ran the tribe. The chief in heaven ran the lesser deities.

Whether the myths and legends were animistic and totemistic as with the Eskimo, the Bantu and others, in which the gods and goddesses take on animal and bird forms which appear to be endowed with immortality, or whether the myths and legends depended on gaints, heroes and demigods as with the Japanese, the Hindu, the Greek or Roman, the collectivist concept was absolute. God was a collective. So was man. It was impossible for early socialist man to imagine anything else.

Early men took note of nature. They saw that animals existed. They thought of themselves as animals. They noticed that animals tended to run in packs. In order for them to kill an animal, they had to separate it from the herd. They concluded, not illogically, that men must herd together and that in the herd was safety. To be banished from the man-herd was the most severe form of punishment meted out by primitive chieftains.

The ancient Hebrews are credited with the first individualization thought processes in known history. But it was not long afterwards when an Egyptian pharaoh got the same idea. However, the idea was not easy for socialists to grasp. Imagine only ONE god, when it is known that man is collective. How could an individualized god control a collectivized creation?

The transition toward individualism was painful and halting. Gradually, the idea arose that not only was there but one God, but all persons were, in the final essence of reality, individuals.

Still the ancient pagan concepts dominated. Believing in the bureaucracy of tribes, even with the revolutionary concept of a single God, early theologians were quick to manufacture a divine bureaucracy. It was against this bureaucracy that Mohammed rebelled, some 600 years after Christ. He reverted to the purity of the "oneness" of each person and the absolute "oneness" of God. He insisted that there "is no God but God." But the concept was too new. In heaven, Mohammed provided places for masters and servants, and managed to push the Almighty into an area of space removed from the deceased who peopled his stratified paradise.

At root, the tribal concept of socialism continued to dominate men's thinking. If it is true that there is only one God, it is manifestly apparent that there is more than one man. Hence, it must be that some men, by virtue of divine right, must rule other men.

But as humankind gropes more and more toward the unfoldment of his potential, it will follow that he will become more individualistic. He will be less willing to accept a bureaucracy whether divine or secular. He will discover his own particular attributes and inclinations and follow them with increasing zeal and determination. As man learns ever more to specialize and to create and conserve great quantities of energy, so he will find that life for him becomes an increasingly flourishing affair. Until this natural direction for the developing species is recognized, man will continue to moor himself to collectivist concepts, either in whole or in part. He will vacillate between the full recognition of himself as a completely unique entity and some half-way unique creature who must be mastered at times by various levels of bureaucratic organization.

The twentieth century brings man to a threshold in his development. Civilization lies through the open doorway. But all about him and deeply imbedded in him are his manifold dependencies upon collectivist concepts. He may elect to move forward despite his fears and his habits of barbarous origin. Or he may elect to move backward and to close the door. But one thing is certain. He cannot stand still. If he would move forward, then he must come to understand his true nature and upon collectivized and socialized criteria.

There are only two ways of obtaining exchanges. One is to rely upon market place exchanges for his desires rather than voluntary, through mutual cooperation in which something can be exchanged for something else. The other is compulsive, wherein cooperation is banished and where some strong man rises to compel exchanges according to a pattern he believes will be beneficial to others or to himself.

In primitive societies, formalized government did not exist as we know it today. Nonetheless, a type of government obtained, usually established by a strong man, a priest or a combination of the two working together. Instead of a body of law there was the body of a man. Obedience rather than voluntary cooperation was the order of the day.

It is the individualistic position that a formalized institution of government is not necessary in order to demonstrate the existence of a governing force. In barbarous communities this governing force flowed from the chief, the priest and from a body of custom, woven into a pattern by taboos and ritual, so that no man dared defy that governing force. The Zunis in Africa felt that they were contaminated if the shadow of an alien to their tribe fell across their food while in preparation or when being eaten. The Bantu saw in virtually every natural event the intrusion of the gods, the presence of the spirits of departed chieftains and the unending authority of their own strong man. To disobey the ritual, the custom or the immediate order of the chief, brought death, immediate, or death through the lingering terror of banishment. In these and other primitive tribes a system of tribal communism or tribal socialism was extant from the earliest times. These savages lived under a condition of TOTAL government. They were controlled in all acts of their lives for they believed in total authority residing outside of themselves personally.

Durant suggests — and it is easy to agree — that civilization begins with the first voluntary action. Under tribal communism, voluntaryism was unknown. But civilization started in some dark time and some remote age where some individualistic savage broke the taboo or violated the custom either by doing something that was forbidden, or by refusing to do something that was commanded. The dawn of civilization broke at that moment. And if Durant is correct respecting the origin of civilization, it is a logical inference that to bring an end to civilization one would simply have to create a society in which all voluntary actions were eliminated — in a word, to establish socialism; to return to barbarism.

We have brought traces of the jungle with us into what we call civilization. That jungle carry-over is our remaining trust and faith in the ancient taboo that government has the ability to control us.

Undoubtedly, an important contribution to the general fallacy is the conclusion of so many historians and philosophers that civilization is, itself, dependent upon government. These savants, including a veritable host of otherwise reasonable and scholarly men, tell us that civilization advances only under the CERTAINTY of LAW. They point to the rise of business and industry in such ancient regimes as Rome's and opine that the single prerequisite of such a burgeoning economy as occurred in the Latin world was the fixed nature of the *corpus juris*. Lacking law, specifically a written and a generally understood law, the market place, these scholars believe, is subjected to the whims of predators against whom the struggling free enterpriser is by all odds outclassed.

Certainty

It is not the nature of the laws so much that concerns these thoughtful men, but the *certainty* of the laws. Civilization and certainty go together, they tell us. If there is no certainty of law, no government to punish some or to reward others, no man knows which pursuit to follow; no man can successfully plan for the future; hence, no possibility of a civilized future unfolds.

On the surface, this argument appears to be valid. But we are in danger here of accepting one fact and one fallacy because we do not permit ourselves to think in a manner void of mythology. Let us agree that certainty and civilization go together. Let us question whether it is government that provides the kind of certainty that civilization requires.

Bruno Leoni, the distinguished Italian professor, in a series of lectures on the subject of freedom and competitive enterprise at Claremont College (California) in 1958, brings us an astonishing reminder. The astonishment proceeds from the fact that the point he makes is so obvious and, until now, so widely overlooked.

We are admonished by the professor to recollect that in ancient Rome there were two bodies of law, that famed *corpus juris* of Justinian which was the legislated body of law; and Roman common law, which was simply a body of custom and usage adopted through the years and ABOVE AND BEYOND THE POWER OF THE SENATE AND THE CAESARS. This common law was the base on which the Roman world rested. It was not written. But it was certain. It was not dependent upon government. It preceded and superseded the formal organization of a body of legal force.

True, the *corpus juris* of Justinian was a latter-day compilation, of which Gibbon ("Decline and Fall of the Roman Empire") was distrustful since there is small evidence to establish the omniscience of Justinian's selection and interpretation of which laws and which decisions were worthy of inclusion in his vast undertaking. Specifically, Justinian belongs to the period of Byzantine ascendancy and thus the Roman compilation of the body of law is actually a by-product, reaching post-historically into a preceding age and time.

Nonetheless, Professor Leoni's position is accurate for one does not require Justinian to ascertain the existence of this body of law. It was a fact. And with it was the additional fact that the unwritten laws, the non-*corpus juris*, provided the bed rock on which the Roman concept of freedom and liberty was based.

We are immediately reminded both of British common law and the American Declaration of Independence. In the former case, during long centuries British subjects grew up in a belief that there were certain rules which applied to them simply because they were British subjects. These rules were not necessarily spelled out by Parliament. They were a part of the common usage and custom, and far more certain than formal, written law.

The British common law dates from most ancient times and generally came about under foreign occupation. It is reasonable to suppose that most persons under the control of outsiders will not willingly obey nor abide by the arbitrary dictations of their foreign masters. Under such duress they tend to gravitate in their sensibilities toward the rugged realities that they face. They find themselves relying upon such natural rules as the Ten Commandments: Thou shalt not murder. Thou shalt not steal. Thou shalt not bear false witness. They will gradually and insensibly oppose dicta which are contrary to these precepts. And since it is true that no government can, in fact, *control* anyone, the foreign invaders are faced with the necessity of reducing their legal enactments to a basis which will ultimately be acceptable to those whom they coerce. This is the basis of British common law.

Referring to the Declaration of Independence, we find the authors and signatories to that document declaring that there are certain rights which precede government and which government cannot take away, among them life, liberty and the pursuit of happiness. By implication, there are others as well.

In addition to rights (functions) which we have universally as a part of our human natures, there is always a body of natural law which is generally understood and which is inherently based upon the Golden Rule. As a matter of natural law we do NOT contravene our rights or functions. It is in this body of natural law that CERTAINTY resides. It can never reside in formalized law, which can be and frequently is contrary to natural law.

Thus, when we examine the precise *function* of government in practice, both in ancient and modern times, we find that governments do NOT provide *certain* law, on which civilization must be based. Rather, governments provide such a welter of conflicting, contradictory, *ever changing* rules, orders, demands, taxes, circumstances, ordinances, codes, prohibitions, subsidies, rewards, and plain red tape, that no man can predict today what the rules are going to be tomorrow.

Thus, if our historians and philosophers are correct, namely, that civilization and certainty go together, it becomes apparent that governments in practice do NOT advance civilization, but raise obstacles across the pathway to such civilization. The only certainty to be traced to government is the uncertainty of governmental conclusions. And when the uncertainty of government in general is augmented by the absolute certainty that government in action will prey upon the persons in the market place, but in such an uncertain and unpredictable manner that no man knows which avenue to pursue or what to avoid, we find that the cause of individualism and hence of civilization, which must invariably rest upon individuals, is thwarted and forestalled.

To quote Professor Leoni: "Even those economists who have most brilliantly defended the free market against the interference of authorities have usually neglected the parallel consideration that no free market is really compatible with a law-making process centralized by the authorities. This leads some of those economists to accept the idea of a certainty of the law, that is, of precisely worded rules as those of written law, which is neither compatible with that of a free market nor, in the last analysis, with that of freedom as the absence of constraint on the part of other people, including authorities, on the private life and business of each individual."

But let us take the modern, and the uniquely American conception that the purpose of the government is to protect the freedom of all. Certainly, this is the most acceptable of the general definitions and the least harmful.

What we are saying here is that government shall have the exclusive power to use force. What we are also saying is that government shall employ that power in a negative way only. Men will be free, unless or until they trespass upon the freedom of another. Then, and then only will the government act. And its actions will be confined to restoring the original state of freedom that has suffered under the transgression.

Protection: Aggressive—Defensive

If this definition is acceptable for the moment, let us proceed. If this is to be the sole function of government, then it would be safe to say that any expansion of the government's power beyond the purely negative protectional functions would be an improper use of that power.

In other words, when the government attempts to build roads, it is not acting in a negative, defensive category. Rather, it is acting in a predatory, socialistic manner by seeking to provide a service which will be used by some of the people, in a manner which will entail taxation of some or all of the people. This is consistent with socialism. And this would be true even if the government collected the money from only some of the people and made the roads available to all of the people. This, too, is socialism, as has been shown. In other words, government roads are socialistic roads.

But this is true up and down the line of governmental operations. In fact, it should be apparent even to the casual thinker that if the government collects money for roads only from those who use the roads, and if anyone can use the roads and in the process pay for their use, then government has invaded the field of private enterprise and is providing a service which can readily be provided by any ambitious and persevering enterpriser. For the same rules apply to admission at a motion picture theater, or any other type of private enterprise. Only those who pay to see the films get to see the pictures. Only those who see the pictures pay for the privilege. Yet the theaters are open to any who wish thus to indulge themselves.

This is free enterprise. If government is limited only to defensive protectionism, then it has no business running motion picture theaters or providing roads. Either would be an invasion of the economy and either would advance the socialist goal of moving what should be private property and private wealth out of private hands and placing that property and wealth into the hands of the government.

This is true from agriculture to zoos, from A to Z.

If the government attempts to provide a product or a service in some other manner than by permitting those who use the product or service to pay for it, to wit, by taxing all so that some may have the service or the product, that in essence is socialism. If, on the other hand, the government seeks to provide a service or product in the same manner as any enterpriser might seek to do the same thing, that is the attainment of the socialist goal which demands that the means of production and distribution be owned and controlled by the state.

Think of anything your government does now. From education to interstate commerce regulation, the classification is the same. Either the government is acting as an enterpriser and thus competing with some legitimate private means of providing goods and services, or it is engaged in a socialist practice of taxing all to provide something for some, or of taxing some to provide something for all.

It can be demonstrated that in all avenues (let us bypass the matter of protection, for the moment) when a government acts, it acts in a socialist manner. It cannot help itself. And again it can be emphasized that the manner or the type of the government, the frequency of elections, if they are held, the blood lines of the rulers, the wealth they enjoy—all of these things are academic distinctions which fail to provide a non-socialist framework in any government. Governments are socialist institutions and have been so from their inception.

Protection

We are left with the sole function of the government a matter of negative defensive force. And now wè face the crowning denouement. For protection is a service in every way comparable to insurance. If a person is compelled to take out insurance, the process is socialistic. If he is compelled to pay for another person's insurance, the process is socialistic. If he receives payments from his insurance that other persons have been compelled to provide, the process is socialistic. And by definition we are faced with the necessity of concluding that even police protection is socialistic.

Some persons wish considerable in the way of police protection. Others see little or no reason for it. But by means of taxation, all pay for it.

Either police protection is a legitimate function of private firms, or it is essentially socialistic. If it is a legitimate free enterprise, then it is simply one more area of human activity in which governments have destroyed competition, by force; and all insurance company inspectors, private guards, night watchmen, railroad detectives, merchant police, private detectives, armored car specialists and so forth, plus the use of burglar alarms, locks on doors and electric eyes, are the rightful guardians of private property and private safety. In this case, governmental intrusion on the scene is an unnatural perversion and should be eliminated just as so many seek to eliminate government competition in other fields.

Otherwise, police protection is essentially socialistic, in which case we must believe that while socialism in all other fields of human need tends always to destroy civilization, a socialist police force operates in the opposite way, to civilize us.

But our problem in viewing protection as a totally negative and defensive function is that in all of known history we have relied upon governments to furnish it. And governments have failed to provide that which we sought.

In fact, governments engaged in protection invariably from the earliest times, buttressed their efforts by establishing courts of competent jurisdiction so that the government's failure to provide protection would not be noted.

Had government protection been successful in fact, the necessity of having a court to adjudicate problems becomes questionable.

This point may be difficult of discernment at first, but let us consider it.

At the moment in these United States, an interesting parallel can be observed. It has become a rather ordinary practice for parents to enroll their children in remedial reading classes. No such classes would be necessary if the children had learned in their normal reading sessions in school. Remedial reading becomes necessary only when reading is not learned when and where it should be learned.

The same observation could be made in connection with defense. If we had provided ourselves with true and adequate defense for our properties or persons, no crimes would ever occur.

Let us be visionary for a moment and imagine a kind of defense that would really defend.

Let us suppose that "A" owns a house. To protect it from arsonists, burglars, robbers, vandals and what not, let us suppose that he contrives an electronic force field which completely (and invisibly) encompasses his building from all sides. Any effort by any individual or group of individuals to break through that defensive shield will result (we will suppose) in the breaking of the miscreant's arm or leg. "A" has merely to throw a switch and his defensive mechanism goes into operation.

Along comes "B," a predator of any kind you choose. "B" makes an effort to get through the shield and finds his arm broken. Does "A" seek to take him to court to prosecute him, to obtain vengeance or other punishment? It would be unlikely. "B" has already suffered the punishment for his criminal intention. "A" might more properly and more likely rush him to a hospital so that the bone could be set. There is no need for vengeance, or retribution of any sort. In fact, it is out of the question. Retribution, if it can be called such, has already occurred because the defensive mechanism WORKED.

When governments preempt the field of protection they invariably fail to provide protection. Rather, they provide extensive and expensive devices by means of which those who have broken through our defenses (thereby proving their ineffectiveness) can be tracked down, prosecuted in court, and, perhaps, ultimately punished. The existence of the court for this purpose is virtual proof of the failure of the defense to work successfully.

Thus, human beings confuse defense with vengeance. They suppose that vengeance is a natural extension of defense when in fact it is only a substitute and is made necessary by the failure of defense to function. But the substitute appears necessary to nearly everyone since the IDEA of adequate defensive measures is almost non-existent.

While it could be argued that governments are the proper and logical devices by means of which vengeance can be taken, it would be difficult or impossible to argue the merits of vengeance if defensive mechanisms truly worked to the point that crimes could not be committed. If a crime can be stopped BEFORE it occurs, by means of adequate defense, then there would be no criminals. A criminal intention to act would carry within itself such enormous risks that the criminal would be pitied rather than pursued in vengeance.

And while admitting that the illustration above of the electronic shield is far fetched and is in the science-fiction tradition, the fact is we do not know what the market place could provide in the way of true defense. By occupying this area of human endeavor, the government has moved all competition out of the field.

We note that whenever a government invades any normal field of human endeavor, the tendency of human beings is to surrender that field and to make no further effort in it. Had market entrepreneurs been free all these ages to examine and explore adequate means of defense rather than relying upon the government to provide it, who can tell what marvelous means of protecting ourselves and our property might now be available to all? And should this field suddenly be opened to man's amazing inventive and productive genius, who can say what might yet ensue? Perhaps the electronic force field is not as far-fetched as one might at first imagine.

While it would be reasonable to claim that any human being has a right to purchase protection for his freedom and for his life and property, it is unreasonable to claim that all must pay for what some want. Logically, police protection is as socialistic when government provides it as are school lunches when government procures, cooks and serves them.

As a matter of fact, any socialist can find an excellent argument here. He can ask, "What is protection?" The word has never been defined with satisfaction to all concerned. Strictly speaking, all government actions are protective. The child receiving a government-provided education is being protected against ignorance. The same child who gets a government-paid-for lunch is being protected against hunger. The farmer with his subsidies is being protected against the vagaries of weather and pestilence and market fluctuations. The inmate of public housing is being protected against the elements. The welfare recipient is being protected against poverty, old age or both. The patient at a government clinic is being protected against ill health. To assume that it is proper and non-socialistic to provide police protection, and at the same time to assume that it is improper and socialistic to provide protection in these other forms, is inconsistent and unrealistic. Protection is protection.

The individualist would claim that protection is a service which should be purchased in the market place like any other service. Those who wish it, should purchase the amount they require and are prepared to pay for. Those who do not wish it at all, should not be coerced into paying for it.

At this point, it is anticipated that the reader may cry out in alarm, the dreadful word ANARCHY! Is not this classification of all acts of government as essentially socialistic in character, a call for the elimination of all government?

If the reader is so inclined he might be reminded that historically the anarchist is simply another socialist, as was pointed out earlier. Issue was taken with the Americana for excluding Proudhon from the socialist classification. Similarly, it might be advisable to recall that the word "government" is a misnomer for the political entity which wields power, for essentially it is the nature of man to govern himself.

Two Types of Law and Order

To emphasize this fact, it is necessary to point out that there are two broad plans for maintaining law and order. One of these is government as it is generally known. The other is also a type of organization, which has demonstrated through the years a superior ability to prevent chaos and to accomplish all manner of human social relationships.

Nor should we become confused by the use of the word "law" in this connection despite the fact that we tend to think of law as the exclusive prerogative of the artificial type of government. Law does not have to be formalized to make it effective. Moral precept, moral law, public opinion are all indications of an active ingredient in the nature of man which counsels a type or pattern of behavior consonant with man's true nature.

For example, most men arise in the morning and go to bed at night. This action is conforming to man's own nature, for man is not a nocturnal animal. But there is no legal fiat that compels this type of action. Custom, public opinion, ordinary usage bring about this pattern in human action. Nor do we throw a man in jail if he violates the pattern.

However, governments have so far intruded into the regulation of man's hours of wakefulness and slumber that already we have legalized "daylight saving time" which arbitrarily sets custom aside and declares for us that during the summer months five o'clock is really six o'clock. Additionally, in some cities there are curfew laws which apply to certain persons, and on occasion to all persons. If artificial government becomes a little more powerful and a little more socialistic, the day may come in which all men will be compelled to arise from their beds at a governmentally determined hour and any variation from this legal directive will be accompanied by the risk of arrest and punishment or the issuance of a special permit to cover the case.

Still, it should be obvious that until such time as the government intervenes, man manages very well, indeed. The normal practice is a pattern or law of behavior. But it is a type of law not enforced by government — at least, not yet.

For the purpose of clarification, these two means of maintaining law and order will be called artificial government and natural government.

What is artificial government?

The term is being used to indicate the type of organization we have in mind whenever we use the word government. Artificial government can consist of any possible combination of authorities whose purpose is to rule, to govern. These combinations include republics, democracies, monarchies, oligarchies, autocracies, theocracies, etc.

What is natural government?

Natural Association

A natural government is rarely called a government. It is a natural association of people who get together not for the purpose of ruling or governing, but for some other purpose, yet whose association brings about a certain type of organizational structure which is conducive to law and order.

There are five principal types of natural government. These are:

1. The family

2. The business group

3. The non-government school

4. The church

5. Any other private organization, club, association or amalgamation

Since these associations are rarely thought of as governing bodies, it is important that their characteristics as governing bodies be understood. The first characteristic should be emphasized. In all natural governments the prime purpose of the association is *not* to govern. In this, the natural associations are in harmony with the laws of man's nature, for man cannot be controlled; he can only control himself. Artificial governments, on the contrary, are invariably organized to accomplish the impossible and the unnatural, namely to control individuals.

The second characteristic of the natural government is that its prime purpose is always desirable to the members, else they do not associate with it. In contrast, the artificial governments have aims which invariably are out of harmony with the desires of a minority of those under their sway. Though they may appeal to a majority in some cases, they will be rejected by some of this same majority in other cases.

The third characteristic is that natural governments rarely attempt and never succeed in bringing all persons within a specific geographic limitation under their sway. The possible exception here is the family and the particular home in which the family lives. But businesses, churches, schools and clubs, however universal their appeal, never succeed in attracting everyone. This is in harmony with man's individualistic nature.

In contrast, an artificial government exercises its power over all within its geographic limits. The geographic limits are first prescribed and all human life within the claimed territory becomes subject to the governors of that territory. This is contrary to the individualistic nature of man.

A fourth characteristic is this: The individual who associates himself in a natural governmental structure of whatever nature, and who then discovers that he is out of harmony with the rules, codes, tenets, policy or aims of that structure, is able to extricate himself from his predicament by the simple process of walking out. And once he is outside the confines, he is not immediately placed under the jurisdiction of some other natural government.

For example, the man who quits his work at the Ford Company does not find, on walking out the door, that he is automatically working for General Motors. The person who stalks from the Methodist Church in anger does not find himself a Catholic. The person who removes himself from the Kiwanis Club does not automatically become a Mason. Each person to so eject himself from some natural organization finds himself in neutral territory. He is free to seek another association. He is free to forego such association.

In contrast, the person under the control of an artificial government may not simply object to the rules and step out. He is not able to step out without the permission and concurrence of the artificial government. And even if he were to succeed in separating himself from that control, he would find that he would have to leave the territory. And leaving the territory he would promptly find himself under the control of another artificial government. In short, there is always escape from the natural governments. There is no escape from the artificial governments.

Still another area of contrast is this: A person who disobeys an edict of a natural government with which he is associated may undergo punishment. But the most extreme form of punishment is, customarily, banishment. The church may oust him; the lodge may blackball him; the boss may fire him. Under an artificial government, death confronts him for disobedience. And even if banishment were to occur, it would only be to move him out from under one governmental control to place him under the domination of another.

In every way it becomes apparent that natural governments operate in conformity to man's true nature and in harmony with the great laws which truly govern all of creation. It is also equally apparent that artificial governments function at cross purposes to nature. Artificial governments inevitably seek to control others; to equalize; to socialize.

Since this line of approach is not generally undertaken, it might be wise to spend a few moments discussing some of the natural types of government. Among the most interesting and most ancient is the family relationship. Let us take it in its ideal form at the beginning.

The Family Relationship

The family begins with two persons, voluntarily agreeing to live and work together. In modern times the male member of the association will presumably be the breadwinner and the female member will presumably be the housekeeper. In economic terms it could be said that the relationship is a free enterprise relationship. The male provides the goods; the female, the services. So long as these goods and services are exchanged on a voluntary basis, the relationship is a free market relationship. And this is true even if the male is not as successful a breadwinner as the female originally imagined, or if the female is not as splendid a housekeeper as the male may have originally anticipated.

Let us suppose there are children. Infants certainly are not physically capable of providing either goods or services in the normal course of events. Are they, then, a violation of the free market relationship? Actually, and still speaking idealistically, they are not such a violation. Although the children may not provide either goods or services, they do provide a type of joy and satisfaction which is compensation enough for their parents. In other words, there is a free exchange in the family unit which is entirely compatible with human rights, human liberty and economic rules of supply and demand.

What we have seen, however, particularly in recent years, is a rise of dependency upon formalized law which affects the free market relationship of members of the family. Let us examine the status of the child primarily.

Some years ago, the family which contained numerous progeny was considered to have an economic advantage in the community. The female children patterned their behavior after their mother. They learned by observation how to weave and sew, how to cook and grind meal, how to clean house and churn butter, and acquired even such refinements as music and song, all from the honorable practice of example. The little girl, even from a very young age, was an advantage around the house. She could look after younger members of the family. She could pitch in with the dusting and cleaning. She could help prepare vegetables and meats for the table. She was an economic asset almost from the start, helping to lift the heavy burden from the hands and shoulders of the distaff side of the family.

And what of the little boy? He, too, became an adjunct to the productive capacities of the family. He trailed his paternal parent to the woods for hunting, to the fields for plowing and cultivating and harvesting. By the time he was seven or eight he was helping. And in his teens he performed as any other man, matching his strength against the might and the experience of his father. Education was by precept and individual patience. Economically, an exchange began as quickly as it could be engineered.

But with the passage of time, laws were passed which presumed that a parent who would ask or urge his offspring to undertake labor of any kind, was cruel or unjust. Rather than permitting the young ones to earn their own way in a market economy, the law prescribed that a child was a dependent. He could not become self-sufficient or even partially self-sufficient without a special permit. Child labor laws helped to socialize the family unit.

Other laws, meanwhile, have corroded the sanctity of the home. The voluntary union of male and female in the ideal sense was buttressed about by legal force which placed enormous coercion in the hands of either mate. Instead of seeking to enrich their own lives by increasing their ability to exchange their goods and services, the emphasis switched to the point where husbands could legally make certain demands upon their wives, and wives could make certain demands upon their husbands. The development of mutual love and understanding was sidetracked into legal areas, with tax-supported "marriage counselors" substituting for the application of ordinary common sense.

Many a wife now believes that she has been socialized because of her husband's position as the breadwinner. She feels dependent, helpless, a victim of a situation she did not dream could exist.

But the male is no less put upon. He believes that his wife has the best of things. He provides, thanks to the creative ability of the market place, wonderful labor-saving devices for her so that the household services she performs are reduced to a minimum. But he believes that legally she has the last word, for he dare not stray away lest she haul him into court and obtain a divorce plus a monthly payment of alimony. The more severe and numerous are the laws enacted to sustain the family unit, the more temptation and pressure that arises to sunder the bonds of matrimony. Surely the incidence of divorce in these United States should establish the prevalence of shattered marriages without undue elaboration here.

Ideally, then, it could be shown that the family unit is a free market relationship, entered into voluntarily and maintained by an exchange of goods, services, satisfactions, joy and

other tangible and intangible rewards, flowing to all members
of the association.

Practically, as time and the law have eroded the relationship, the family unit has become, at least so far as children are
concerned, largely socialistic, with some elements of socialism
(perhaps) adhering even to the basic male and female relationship. But this is caused by the intrusion of government force
into what would otherwise remain a free and voluntary association.

The strong opposition to the family provided by Plato,
Marx and the modern "do-gooders" via legal decrees, gives
us indication enough that the free market family unit is the
core of the opposition to the socialist program. So long as voluntary, free market exchanges occur between men, women
and children, the socialist program will fall short of fulfillment.[1]

1. Engels gives credit to Lewis Morgan, anthropologist, for Marx's
   position respecting the family. In his study, "Ancient Society,"
   Morgan establishes that our concept of the family relationship is
   the modern concept and has not always been prevalent. Morgan
   traces family relationships through five steps: The Consanguine
   Family; The Punaluan Family; The Syndyasmian Family; The
   Patriarchal Family; The Monogamian Family. (cont. on page 260)

At the present moment the family is under severe attack; its authority and influence undermined by the socialized government schools; by socialized legislation which prohibits child labor; by government clinics, juvenile courts, marriage counselors and a host of other devices.

It is almost invariably shocking to the parent to learn, for example, that the abolition of child labor and the rise of government schools are an integral part of the communist program and among the basic dream components of the socialist fiction. "Free education for all children in public schools. Abo-

He shows that the two earliest forms date from barbarism, that the next two forms are transitional and result finally in the Monogamian family, which is the modern form.

Marx accepted the Morgan thesis largely because of the inference drawn by Morgan that it is only with the Monogamian family that the concept of private property is possible.

"The growth of the idea of property in the human mind, through its creation and enjoyment, and especially through the settlement of legal rights with respect to its inheritance, are intimately connected with the establishment of this form (Monogamian) of the family. Property became sufficiently powerful in its influence to touch the organic structure of society."

Marx, convinced that he must destroy the concept of private ownership, was quick to rally his arguments to oppose the modern family.

lition of children's factory labor in its present form. Combination of education and industrial production," etc., etc. (Communist Manifesto, point 10.)

Socialist Family Objectives

It is equally shocking for parents to learn that this program was in vogue in this country before Karl Marx was born. The first assumption of state responsibility for the education of children occurred in Massachusetts in 1648, only 28 years after the successful founding of the Plymouth Colony.

But while we are on the subject of the family it might serve to bring out the socialist argument as Marx sets it down:

"Abolition of the family! Even the most radical flare up at this infamous proposal of the Communists.

"On what foundation is the present family, the bourgeois family, based? On capital, on private gain. In its completely developed form this family exists only among the burgeoisie. But this state of things finds its complement in the practical absence of the family among the proletarians, and in public prostitution.

"The bourgeois family will vanish as a matter of course when its complement vanishes, and both will vanish with the vanishing of capital.

"Do you charge us with wanting to stop the exploitation of children by their parents? To this crime we plead guilty.

"But, you will say, we destroy the most hallowed of relations, when we replace home education by social.

"And your education! Is not that also social, and determined by the social conditions under which you educate, by the intervention, direct or indirect, of society by means of schools, etc.? The Communists have not invented the intervention of society in education; they do but seek to alter the character of that intervention, and to rescue education from the influence of the ruling class.

"The bourgeois clap-trap about the family and education, about the hallowed co-relation of parent and child, becomes all the more disgusting, the more, by the action of modern industry, all family ties among the proletarians are torn asunder, and their children transformed into simple articles of commerce and instruments of labor.

"But you Communists would introduce community of women, screams the whole bourgeoisie in chorus.

"The bourgeois sees in his wife a mere instrument of production. He hears that the instruments of production are to be exploited in common, and naturally, can come to no other conclusion, than that the lot of being common to all will likewise fall to the women.

"He has not even a suspicion that the real point aimed at is to do away with the status of women as mere instruments of production.

"For the rest, nothing is more ridiculous than the virtuous indignation of our bourgeois at the community of women, which, they pretend, is to be openly and officially established by the Communists. The Communists have no need to introduce community of women; it has existed almost from time immemorial.

"Our bourgeois, not content with having the wives and daughters of their proletarians at their disposal, not to speak of common prostitutes, take the greatest pleasure in seducing each others' wives.

"Bourgeois marriage is in reality a system of wives in common, and thus, at the most, what the Communists might possibly be reproached with, is that they desire to introduce, in substitution for a hypocritically concealed, an openly legalized community of women. For the rest, it is self-evident that the abolition of the system of production must bring with it the abolition of the community of women springing from that system, i.e., of prostitution both public and private." (Communist Manifesto)

This is Plato preserved in vitriol.

Clearly, the author of these words and his multiplying followers in and out of the Fabian camp, have little conception of marriage as a relationship which contains other attributes than a license for sexual indulgence. The socialist is seen here in his most social and his least economic position. The complete alteration of the social structure is under his guns.

The individualist is not so constituted. He views marriage as a voluntary relationship which is based on a free market exchange and, additionally, contains a host of other elements that make life worth the living. He sees in the family a reservoir of love, devotion, sanctity, sacrifice, cooperation, self-discipline and progress.

To their credit, the Fabians have soft-pedaled family reform publicly. Still, the advance of the Fabian juggernaut through the medium of the public school, public clinic, public welfare, child guidance, juvenile courts, and so on, has quietly done much to undermine parental authority and influence. The family unit today is under severe attack and if it is to be preserved, it will be because, despite the Marxian arguments, it is superior to the state in providing a safeguard and a haven for our offspring.

Let us once more underline the fact that the family is a voluntary unit. One parent may exercise a type of authority over all other members of the family. But the punishment of a child for disobedience is tempered by the parental role and does not lead to death. And the purpose of the parental role is not to perpetuate childhood but to prepare the child for maturity. Thus, in contradistinction to all artificial governments, with the passage of time the authority over the child wanes. The infant may be dominated at each instant, the small child at frequent intervals. But the youth receives only occasional guidance, and the mature youth properly breaks away from the family of his rearing and seeks his own fortune as a free being. There is nothing in this relationship which is opposed to nature. On the contrary, this is the fulfilling of man's nature.

Business Relationships

Let us consider the business establishment. This, too, provides a type of natural government. The manager, whether an individual, a family, a board of directors or a partnership, exercises a type of authority over all other members of the establishment. Management provides the rules and the laws which all must obey. Failure to obey will result in banishment, but never in imprisonment or death. And, again, the association is voluntary. Before a person can join a business establishment, a mutual agreement must be reached. The employee finds that he can and will perform certain services or provide certain skills. The management finds that it will accept those services or skills and pay the employee in money or in some other way acceptable to both parties. Failure to reach an agreement means that the individual will not become an employee. Agreement reached means that an exchange between the management and the employee will be undertaken according to terms and conditions agreed upon beforehand.

This, too, is in keeping with the nature of things. There is no violation here either of economic rules or of natural law; the association is wholly voluntary. It can be broken off at any time by either party.

These same conditions would be manifested in any kind of voluntary club or organization. (Note: Unions cannot be classed as voluntary.) They would also pertain in any private institution such as a school or a church which was not under government control or domination.

It is normal and natural for human beings to join forces for purposes of accomplishing specific objectives. So long as the joining together is accomplished without duress and so long as a condition of voluntary exchange exists, there is no harmful socialism. The damage occurs, and it can occur in any natural government, whenever the natural and normal voluntary relationship is breached by the intrusion of force. The employee whose employer is forced to pay him a "minimum" wage has been socialized in that area. The member of the union who is forced to join and to pay dues, and to contribute to the welfare or pension fund, has been socialized, and the sums of money taken from such a member will inevitably be used in furthering socialist objectives, either through political or social action. These instances of violence and coercion, however, are departures from the norm.

It is interesting to note that by far and away all rules and laws which govern society are formulated under these private and natural agencies. These associations build the moral code and social custom. On the contrary, all artificial governments function in a manner wholly unnatural and disdainful of human rights. Under the rules promulgated by an artificially devised governing power, a minority will inevitably be oppressed. Disobedience to governmental edict is punishable by fine or imprisonment. And in the event of ultimate disobedience, the rebel can be shot down in his tracks.

What should be seen is that the natural agencies which manage and conduct the affairs of mankind with outstanding success, contrive to keep order, provide for the livelihood, the pleasure, the education, the morality, and the general advancement of the race, and they do all these things with a minimum of cost and a maximum of result.

Still, the artificial agencies are employed which endeavor to control human beings, which is contrary to the nature of human life; they perform with a notable lack of success, and through the years, aside from stirring up strife and discord, they produce minimal results for maximum cost.

Business Conspiracies

While we are engaged in a discussion concerning business as a natural agency, we may as well conduct an excursion into the often repeated accusation that businessmen are not to be trusted. Let us concede that businessmen are human; they are subject to error; they are motivated by self-interest; and they are not above questionable practices.

It is not that men in business are a superior KIND of men compared to men in government. It is rather that men in business, in order to succeed, MUST practice a kind of discipline and self-control whereas their counterparts in government may find it to their political advantage NOT to practice discipline and self-control in the same degree or manner.

The man who works for success in business must satisfy his customers in a superior fashion. Even while selfishly motivated, he can only hope for success by superior performance which pleases customers. Assuming a free market in which customers can express their preferences, the businessman must win the support of his customers every day. If he fails to please them, they will switch loyalties and patronize his competitor. Hence, he must always be engaged in seeking to improve his product and to lower its price at the same time he makes his service better. Only by doing these things can he win customers, who are always free to forsake him.

The same man in political office would find an entirely different set of elements with which to contend. He must please a majority of persons during an election. This can be done readily on the basis of promises made. He does not have to deliver on the basis of his promise. The record of broken political promises speaks for itself.

Once in office, the pleasing of his constituents is not a prime consideration. Until the next election the job of ousting him from office is so difficult as to render the process almost obsolete. And when the next election comes, he can always blame his failures to keep his promises on the political opposition.

He can, in the interim, operate on the basis of authority with or without individual consent. He can, and frequently does, alienate many individuals in the course of his career. But his support is collective, his opposition is individual. And he can exert the power of his office to extend favors, to deal in patronage, to cater to large groups so that even though he may injure many as individuals, this fact need not adversely affect him in the next ballot contest.

But let us suppose that a group of businessmen enter into a conspiracy to fix prices or to limit wages. The accusation is frequently made. What would happen?

During the reign of Louis XIV of France a group of Paris businessmen met for the purpose of setting a maximum rate for wages. These business leaders agreed that wage rates were rising; the superior worker was becoming hard to deal with, demanding ever more money; it would be "good for business" if the major business concerns agreed among themselves that wages should never be permitted to rise above such and such a figure.

Unanimously, the leaders agreed. When the meeting adjourned, several of the businessmen who had attended were the first to break the provisions of the agreement. Believing the other businessmen would be bound by the terms of the understanding, they quickly sought out a few superior workmen and offered them higher wages in order to win a competitive advantage. The effort to set maximum wages came to naught.

And this is only one illustration of a sequence of events that has repeated again and again without noticeable variation. Businessmen MUST compete. Although they may weep bitter tears over what they term "unfair" competition, they will still take any advantage that they can take competitively, in order to please their customers a little more.

But there is a more melancholy note to be heard. Businessmen, finding that they did NOT stay bound to voluntary agreements of this nature, did try to develop ways and means of binding other businessmen permanently and without recourse. Businessmen did organize to persuade or pressure government to enact special bits of legislation to protect their own businesses (tax rebates, tax moratoria, tax exemptions) or to interfere with the businesses of others (tariffs, allocations, priority lists, embargoes).

Here we see the businessman forsaking the market place and the natural laws which rule there, hying himself to the government and the artificial restraints and compulsions which abound there. This is a great evil.

Let us not blame the men in government or the men in business for this. Men are men and they are strange composite creatures containing individually much good and much bad.

If we can, through education, teach free market economics; if we can understand the nature of man and the nature of man's government; then through knowledge we can yet learn to avoid government interference in the economy and to rely upon free market, voluntary actions.

Were the government incapable of stepping into the market place to favor some at the expense of others, no monopoly or "cornering" the market could take place. Whatever the intentions of men may be, if they are impotent to secure exclusive privilege we have little to fear from them.

The government is a weapon ever at hand by means of which man can set other men against one another. The instrument itself is the embodiment of this kind of evil. It should be abandoned for this purpose.

The Nature of Competition

Most of us object to monopoly. We dislike the idea that any one person or firm would have so much control over any commodity or resource that all others would be barred.

Yet, curiously, we trust government, which must be a monopoly. And we tend to distrust the market place, where monopoly cannot occur without government intervention.

The supposition exists that an individual or a group of them operating exclusively along free market lines not only can, but probably would tend to establish a monopoly. Indeed, many persons contend that one of the principal services a government can provide is to be on hand to prevent the formation of monopolies or, at least, to break them up if and when they do occur. It was because of such thinking that the Sherman anti-trust law was first put on the books. It was because of an extension of this same fallacy that the Clayton act followed.

To understand the real nature of monopoly in the market place, one must first understand there are four kinds of competition. Each of these types of competition is natural and will exist unless or until government curtails or eliminates it. The four kinds of competition are as follows:

1. Direct competition.

This is the kind of competition which occurs between the Ford Motor Company and the Chrysler Motor Company. Both firms make automotive vehicles in a number of styles, sizes and colors. They compete directly for the same customers. They appeal to customers on the basis of price, service, firm reputation, innovations, color, style, and a number of variables. There are thousands of other illustrations of direct competition.

2. Parallel competition.

This is the kind of competition which occurs between the General Motors Corporation and Chris Craft. Or between Chris Craft, Beechcraft and General Motors. All of these firms are interested in transportation. They are competing for customers, but not necessarily the same customers in each case. The man who buys a Buick may elect to drive from Chicago to Buffalo, New York. The man who buys a Chris Craft may elect to go through the Great Lakes to the same destination. The man who buys a Beechcraft may elect to fly from Chicago to Buffalo. All firms here deal in transporting human beings. But each has its own sphere of operation and its own sphere of influence.

Perhaps a better illustration of parallel competition would be found in public transportation. We have bus lines, railroads, barge lines and airlines, all vying for the customer's dollar, both in passenger and freight traffic.

Still another illustration would be found in the entertainment field, i.e., theaters, moving pictures, dance halls, carnivals, circus performances, television, radio. In the advertising business there are equally valid examples of parallel competition: newspapers, radio stations, television stations, magazines, billboards, direct mail, etc. Competition between parallel competitors can be just as vigorous and keen as competition between direct competitors.

3. Dollar competition.

Economics deals always with things that are valuable because of scarcity. Inflated though our currency is, the dollar is still of value because it is in short supply. Let everyone have all the dollars he can possibly spend and the dollar would quickly have no value. All persons in business are competing with all other persons in all other businesses, for dollars. There is always a short supply of dollars. The man who buys an umbrella may not have enough dollars on hand to buy a new hat as well. The lady who gets a permanent wave may have to go without a new pair of shoes. The child who gets to see the latest full-length western may have to forego the ice cream sundae. This, too, is competition.

4. Finally, invisible competition.

This is the most difficult to see, but it is one of the most powerful forces to operate in the market place. Let us assume, for the sake of illustrating our point, that A has established a bakery in the town of Y. It is the only bakery there. It has what some would call a monopoly position.

Let us suppose A has done such a superior job of providing bread and other baked goods for the citizens of Y that even the housewives stop buying flour because they can get better products from A for less money.

A is certainly in an advantageous position. He has no direct competition. Even his parallel competition is waning. Dollar competition continues, of course. This is invariably present unless government intrudes and compels purchase of a competitor's goods.

Now, is there anything to prevent A from raising his prices sky high (the invariably expressed fear of monopoly) and thus make a financial killing on all the inhabitants of Y?

Yes, there is. The deterrent is what we call "invisible competition."

In the market place there are two signals which fly invisibly above every place of business. One of these is the flag of price; the other, the flag of quality-service.

Every person interested in going into business or in expanding existing business is always on the alert for those two flags. If he observes that the price flag of a given business begins to rise, he watches that business to see when he will be able to break into the business in competition with an advantage to himself.

If he sees the flag of quality-service starting to come down the flagstaff, he is similarly motivated. The place where the entrepreneur does not dare intrude is at the place where the price flag is low and the quality-service flag is high. When the reverse occurs, assuming a free market and no government interference, entrance of direct competition is certain.

What happens in the village of Y, then, when A's baker does a superb job? One of two things occurs if the market is free. Mr. A continues to keep his price flag low and his quality-service flag high, thus showing he recognizes the chance of a real competitor if he does anything else. He is competing against the invisible competitor — the free market man who would be there the minute he slackened his vigilance.

If Mr. A seeks to take advantage of his position by lowering his quality-service flag or by raising his price flag, or both, he will find that he is no longer competing against an invisible competitor, for his competition will have become real and tangible.

This is the nature of competition in the market place. Only government, with its ability to tax, to padlock, to erect tariff barriers, to provide allocations of scarce materials, to grant exclusive franchises, and in the end to compel payment, can prevent competition from acting in some if not all of its normal ways of acting.

We should have no fear of the market place if we fear monopoly. Competition is the natural resident of all free markets. Monopoly and special privilege are the prerogatives of governments only.

No Harmful Socialism Without Force

Socialism in its virulent and harmful compulsive form is totally dependent upon the artificial agency. There could be no socialism in any harmful capacity were it not for the government.

It would appear that the best way to offset the present trend toward socialism would be to acquaint human beings with their own true nature and encourage them to be independent of artificial government to as large a degree as possible.

Marxism and Fabianism are impossible devices for attaining the socialist dream unless government force is used. It is useless and worse than futile to attack socialists as individual people. Almost all people are attracted to socialism in some degree. The only possible means of avoiding the collapse of our present civilization under the pressures of socialist parasitism, is through education.

CHAPTER 12

RETURN OF THE HYDRA

There are a number of superior works in existence treating with the economics of socialism. Since this book does not purport to be primarily either an economic study or an argument in support of freedom in the economic field, the area has been vacated in favor of other works. Economics has been touched upon only briefly in preceding chapters. In summation of the economic syllogism, it is sufficient if we merely emphasize that man does not produce without incentive, and that the hope and expectation of gain is a far stronger incentive than the fear of punishment or death.

The free market gives us the first incentive; socialism, when it is politically activated, gives us the second. If socialism is attempted sans political means, we have a relatively harmless form of voluntary share-the-wealth and share-the-poverty. From the standpoint of production, even though the association may be voluntary, it is not conducive of the most pleasing results. When individuals herd together, the tendency is for no one of the herd to exert himself unduly. It is only when private ownership is implicit and when rewards are commensurate with effort expended, that superior effort will be made. Life on this planet requires superior effort. Survival may be possible without superior effort, but mere subsistence and true progress are scarcely comparable conditions.

A sound argument can be made in the economic field to abandon sharing as a principle, and rely upon individual freedom and individual effort. This, properly, should be the subject of another work or, better yet, of other authors.

Recommended Studies

The reader is referred to such splendid contemporary works as "Human Action" by Ludwig von Mises, and his "Planned Chaos," "Socialism" and "The Anti-Capitalistic Mentality." Additional support for the free enterprise position can be found in William Paton's "Shirtsleeve Economics," Henry Hazlitt's "Economics in One Lesson," and F. A. Harper's "Liberty — A Path To Its Recovery" and "Why Wages Rise."

It remains for us then to examine the nature of political action or political force, and to recognize that whatever its character and however it is formed, an artificial government is an instrument of political force and coercoin.

But now we must ask the question: Is a use of force inevitably a violation of moral law? The answer appears to be it is not. It is not possible to believe in private ownership without endowing the owner of private property with a right to protect that which is his. All persons would have this right in equal amount. All persons have a right to protect and defend their own lives and their own property.

It is not force, per se, that is immoral. It is force used aggressively that is immoral. The individual who employs defensive force is well within his moral rights. In other words, the use of violence is only justifiable on moral grounds when the violence is employed to meet and to cope with *a priori* violence. The aggressor cannot justify his action; the defender can.

But the answer requires a most careful splitting of hairs. This is most treacherous ground on which to stand for it is almost impossible to draw the line between the two types of force, although in the abstract they can readily be discerned. By a definitive process, it would be possible to draw a line and to insist that when force is used by one to cross that line, the action is aggressive and that when the victim counters with force which hurls the attacker back to the line and no further, then defensive force has come into play. But by the same process, if the defender in turn crosses the line in an effort to put down aggression, he is himself committing it. The dilemma which follows any effort to discover when defensive force becomes aggressive, or when aggression becomes defense, is profound and extensive.

Here are two men. One calls the other an unpleasant name. The second retaliates in kind. The first issues a threat of violence. The second presents an even more wicked threat. The first shakes his fist. The second stoops to pick up a stone. The first grabs a stick. The second throws the stone but misses, intentionally. The first swings his stick and connects with the second's head, unintentionally. The violence is now joined.

Will someone kindly draw the line that separates defensive from aggressive force in this hypothetical illustration?

Only in theory can we argue about such niceties. In practice, force is force. Now, in theory, if we can determine who started the aggression we can justify the defense. In practice, there are no aggressors. In warfare every hostile act is retaliatory.

A useful illustration of aggressive and defensive force in contrast, is provided by the well-known "Merchant of Venice" by William Shakespeare. Antonio, the merchant, is in desperate straits for ready cash. He borrows from Shylock the sum of 3,000 ducats, on a ninety-day note. The note is secured not in the normal manner but by a grant to Shylock of the privilege of cutting off a pound of flesh from over Antonio's heart in the event the note is not paid in full on or before the due date.

Essentially, the contract, though unusual, is voluntary on both sides. No one compels Antonio to borrow the money. No one compels him to agree to such bizarre terms. No one compels Shylock to lend the money. The two men are each serving their own interests and the relationship thus far is wholly within the confines of the market place.

But as sometimes occurs, Antonio is unable to meet the obligation within the time specified and Shylock is thus in a position to collect his bond of a pound of flesh.

The situation has now developed to a point where aggression is inevitable. Either Shylock will collect — his contractual privilege — and in the process commit a physical act of assault upon his debtor, or Antonio will take steps to prevent the collection, thereby violating Shylock's contractual prerogatives.

Shakespeare solves the problem by suggesting in Portia's speech that there is a higher law than simple contractual justice, namely, mercy. At this point Shylock abandons the part of villainy and says that he will now be happy with the money and will not press the enactment of the forfeiture clause in the bond. Shakespeare might have contented himself with this, causing Antonio to pay the loan, and all might have ended on a harmonious note. But Shakespeare had to carry the villainy all the way. Therefore, he has Portia play the part of a Daniel backed by *lex talionis*.

It now seems that in spite of the fact that the original bond was voluntarily joined on both sides, it can be construed as representing a plot on Shylock's part to take the life of Antonio. In any place but a stage courtroom, this would be absurd, since Shylock, though he may have hated Antonio, could scarcely be devious in an open, voluntary agreement. Both ran a risk, the one with the loss of his money, the other with the loss of his life.

But, since this is high drama, the audience, cheated of a chance to see Antonio's blood, at least expects the next best thing. Therefore, Shylock is ruined by the court, his goods and wealth forfeited, and Antonio, who actually does owe the money, is excused from paying it. This is aggression and violence against Shylock, but the audience loves it and will join in cheering when the luckless loan shark is driven to suicide.

Some veterans of the theatre say that their sympathies have always been with Shylock. Good for them. Shakespeare did not write the play that way nor intend that it be so interpreted.

Assuming a situation in real life wherein a merchant was in desperate circumstances for a loan, if he had the necessary security he could pledge it against his borrowings. And in the event of default, his securities would be forfeited and no aggression would have occurred at all.

Thus, by means of Shylock's call to enforce his contract, we should learn that when defense exceeds the requirements of justice, it may in turn become aggression.

Aggression and Defense

The problem is in discovering that somewhat mystic line of demarcation between defense and aggression. If someone attempts to knock you down, clearly you have a right to prevent him from doing so. But you would have no right to shoot him. To return an aggressive assault which we might arbitrarily assess as containing 10 ergs of energy, with a defense move containing 100 ergs of energy, would cause the defense to become offense by 90 ergs.

So we are left with the moral conviction that we have a right to defend ourselves, but we face the practical fact that such defense, unless precisely controlled and limited, may constitute a use of aggressive force.

The use of aggressive force constitutes an immoral action. The use of defensive force can be justified on moral grounds. But the problem of defining objectively the difference between aggressive and defensive force in each instance is thus far beyond our powers of scientific measurement.

But let us continue in the moral vein. Whether or not we can always delineate defensive force, the fact would remain that man should have a right to defend himself and it would appear that he equally has a right to select his weapons of defense. Thus, in this theory, no weapon is barred the defender. He may use any weapon at all — guns or other instruments of killing; lying, cheating or deceit; or he could even use the ballot box and socialistic devices for the purpose of defeating a political program which he deemed harmful to him. Of course, since the defender has a right to select his own weapons of defense, he might elect to employ no weapon at all. But this is another story.

It might be proper to inquire whether the use of such defensive weapons as lies, theft and killing can be justified morally at all. Even though it is morally right to defend one's self, it is possible that the use of the weapons of defense may have a destructive result upon the character of the person who employs such weapons. Actually, it is difficult to hold a man in high esteem who lies to protect himself. It may be that at income tax time many people do this very thing and justify it, too. But practice with any weapon tends to create skill in the use of the weapon. And the killer who employs a gun in his own defense, not infrequently perishes by his own device.

Whether or not he dies under arms, the use of a gun for defense tends to make him skillful with the weapon; the use of a lie for his own defense tends to make him a skillful liar; and the use of cheating or deceit in his own defense tends to make him a skillful cheat. Once a skill is acquired, it is increasingly difficult not to employ the skill in areas other than defense. The problem mounts.

We are concerned fundamentally with socialism. And the problem of socialism is condensed to read that socialism poses an economic threat of universal sharing brought on by the coercion and violence of government, which can and does compel such sharing.

To combat this threat, which would not exist were it not for governmental participation, thousands of persons have endeavored to band together to take political action. Essentially, their position is one of defense, and hence can be justified on moral grounds. The socialist, to the person who believes in the sanctity of private ownership, is a thief. The practical problem, then, is: How can the pro-private ownership group combat the political intrigue of the Fabians and Marxists without employing political intrigue as a defensive weapon? Many thousands feel that to avoid political intrigue as a defensive weapon would be tantamount to surrender. And surely, even at this late date, surrender is unthinkable.

It is possible to advance a moral argument against the use of political intrigue. But since the individualist is committed to the rights of private ownership and of self-defense, such an argument would be most difficult for him to marshal. Rather than advancing a moral argument here, let us content ourselves with an argument based upon practical deductions. Surely, few will seek to claim that an unwillingness to employ political intrigue is immoral. Let us view political intrigue outside the moral theater. Let us view it not as either moral or immoral, but rather as it may or may not affect the practical results of the conflict between the individualist and the socialist.

Seeking a Solution

Let us open this part of our study by reviewing the fact that politically speaking, our major danger comes from the Fabian approach.

We do not have to concern ourselves with anarchy. The anarchist, though he is economically ignorant and wishes a shared abundance and poverty, is not one who seeks to employ politics for his own ends. Rather, he is a political individualist, seeking to minimize, reduce or even to do away with government.

The Marxian approach, we will recall, centers on revolutionary devices to overthrow existing social conditions and intends replacing existing government by a type of democratic regime which theoretically is responsive to the will of the proletariat. But Marxism is not nearly so potent a threat as is supposed in many places. To begin with, it is too violent, too militant to awaken wide support. Most people are not revolutionists. Most people wish to make their own way in peace without participating in street fighting, picketing and cloak and dagger work. Further, one can count on the officials in almost any government banding together to put down revolt against that government.

There may be traitors who arise from time to time within the framework of a specific government who seek to cause its overthrow. But simple self-preservation will usually spur the non-traitors in that same government to coalesce their energies, to enact whatever laws are needful, to arm themselves if necessary, and to oust the villainous subverters. Should they fail to take these steps they have only themselves to blame, for the power is in their hands to accomplish such an objective.

Our problem relates not to what they do in respect to traitors and subverters within their own ranks, but to the absolute necessity of retaining our rights and our property outside of the political framework. In short, government's problems of self-preservation are and remain a problem within the government. The problem of the individual, which is also self-preservation, is to insure that his government does not destroy his ability to preserve either his life or his property. Therefore, there is an inevitable conflict, ordained by the laws of nature itself, between individuals outside of government who wish to survive and persons inside government who wish to maintain a given governmental framework and who prey upon the taxpayers outside of government to accomplish their end.

Marxism, which counts on this head-on collision between the ruling class and the proletariat, might be more of a threat than it is were it not that the socialists have found a better way than to rely upon the results of the collision.

It is Fabian gradualism that is our central problem. For by the Fabian bridge to socialism, any enlargement in the size of government is a victory for socialism; any increase in taxation, any taking of property or the control of property, any subsidizing, any business operation by government — any of these steps advances the socialist Fabian toward his ultimate aim and objective.

Therefore, from a practical point of view, the problem now comes into focus. Examples are available to illustrate the danger of fighting Fabianism by means of politics.

You Can't Win for Losing

It may be recalled that in 1958 during a particularly active three-month period, hosts of anti-socialists wrote their government demanding a cut in taxes. This was one of the heaviest inundations of mail the various Congressmen had ever received. So heavy did the mail become, in fact, that a measure was proposed which approved the hiring of an additional administrative assistant for each member of the lower House. Each administrative assistant was to earn $10,000 a year. Each had as his specific duty, the answering of the mail of the Congressmen in whose office he was employed.

The necessity for hiring the additional personnel was occasioned by the demands of conservatives who wanted a cut in taxes. The result of the demand would have increased taxes by just short of $5,000,000 per year to process the objections to higher taxes.

The Hoover Commission performed herculean service during the first and the second periods of its activity. The final report issued by the Citizens Committee for the Hoover Report indicated more than 70 per cent of the economy policies urged by this commission had been approved and made into law, either through legislative action or through executive action.

Certainly, Herbert Hoover's integrity and desire are not open to question. He and some 700 experts produced a series of recommendations which were published in an extensive library numbering more than three score volumes. In all, it took more than 5,800,000 words to explain and describe the research that went into this endeavor. The Hoover Commission was originally launched in 1947 and didn't wind up its affairs until the final report of the Citizens Committee in October of 1958. Thus, it served for eleven years.

There are eight major contributions to economy in government claimed by the committee. These are:

1. The Military Unification Act of 1949.

2. Creation of the General Services Agency which combined four previous agencies.

3. Complete reorganization of the State Department internally.

4. Consolidation of the functions in a Labor Department of full Cabinet stature.

5. The end of political appointments in the corruption-ridden Bureau of Internal Revenue, which now operates under the merit system.

6. Regrouping of welfare activities and the creation of the Department of Health, Education and Welfare.

7. Separation of "hidden subsidies" from the payments for carriage of airline mail.

8. Elimination of much delay, waste and duplication in the Post Office.

These are the claims to greatness of the Hoover workers. Again be it noted that these citizens labored diligently and earnestly to bring about economy, the elimination of waste and duplication of effort.

In candor, however, let us admit the truth. The economies intelligently, even scientifically determined by this dedicated group have not resulted in economy nor in a shrinking in the size or the power of the general government. The record shows two things:

1) A major part of all recommendations were accepted and have been implemented;

2) Government size has continued to expand with each passing year, and taxes have continued to rise.

The Labor Department is now more efficient and costly than before. The Military Unification of the Armed Services has boosted our budget to an annual $40 billions from less than $30 billions when the commission began working. The new Cabinet Department of Health, Education and Welfare is sponsoring some of the most enormous drives for spending and squandering ever sponsored in this nation. The Post Office has not unloaded its deficit and postal rates have been raised.

In short, in the very areas where the Hoover Commission labored most ardently, growth and cost have increased. It seems that when a government agency is operated in a loose and wasteful manner, growth and extravagance are the rule. But when the agency is disciplined and streamlined, while it may eliminate waste, it becomes more efficient, grows even more alarmingly, and requires even more money.

One further illustration should serve. From the beginning of the "New Deal" under Roosevelt until it culminated in the political victory of 1952, the Republicans labored valiantly to stem the tide of socialism which had obviously penetrated the ranks of the party of Jefferson. But when Mr. Eisenhower went to the White House, the only noticeable change in the political climate was that the socialism which had permeated the Republican camp then became visible. There has been no appreciable change in political direction since 1932.

In point of fact, there has been no change in political direction since 1789. Even Jefferson cried out against the manner in which the federal powers were enlarging and the presumed safeguards of state sovereignty were being undermined.

"But the federal branch has assumed in some cases, and claimed in others, a right of enlarging its own powers . . . . retained to the independent branches, mere interpolations into the compact, and direct infractions of it." (Solemn declaration and protest of the Commonwealth of Virginia, written by Jefferson, on the principles of the Constitution of the United

States of America, and the violations of them, December, 1825. "The Complete Jefferson," Tudor Publishing Co., N. Y.)

The business of politics has been the single business in the United States which, from the inception of the nation, has never truly experienced a depression. Though there have been periods of relative calm, the government in the main has continued to grow larger and more costly with each passing year.

Enlargement Inevitable

This growth has been contrary to the intentions and the wishes of great numbers of people in this nation. Even those who vote in such a manner that they oppose an enlargement of government, inadvertently assist in enlarging it anyway, on the simple basis that their own participation makes the government that much more important and that much more costly, whatever the result of any particular election.

We are faced with the problem that confronted Hercules in his twelve labors. Sent to the marshes of Lerna by Argos, Hercules was required to slay the nine-headed hydra. His problem almost got the better of him, for every time he cut off a head, two more grew in its place. Hercules, with the assistance of Iolaus, finally figured out what to do. Cutting off a head was not sufficient. The roots had to be burned out. And then, since one head was immortal and couldn't be slain, they buried that one under a rock.

So, if we may compare the American political scene to the labors of Hercules, it could be suggested that our problem is not simply to vote against socialism, but to burn out the roots. And should it prove that one of the heads of the monster is immortal, a rock must be found under which to bury it.

At the moment, every time we seek to lop off one of the heads of our own governmental hydra, two more grow in its stead. Clearly, the reason for this is that we imagine that by employing the socialism of government against some particular kind of socialism being advocated by government, we can eliminate socialism. Clearly, we cannot. So long as we employ the weapon of government to perform services for us, we will have to pay for the use of that weapon.

The only course open to us relates to the socialism within each of us. Since each one of us controls his own energy and cannot possibly control the energy of any other human being, it is futile to organize to fight socialism. Organization of this kind creates a social unit and tends to nullify the effectiveness of the individual.

One can scarcely oppose collectivism by embracing collectivism. Yet the collective can never conquer the individual for the simple reason that nature has seen to it that only individuals can control their own energy.

Our problem, then, begins and ends with ourselves and not with government. The process is one which involves education and not elections, as Plato properly saw, although he was looking in an opposite direction. If each of us can elevate our own minds; if each of us can discipline our own desires; if each of us can extend maximum efforts into the field of production and distribution; if each of us can practice freedom and support individualistic and capitalistic free enterprise, socialism will have no chance at all.

Socialism's big opportunity always comes when we as individuals give up the struggle and turn to the government to do things for us which we should properly do for ourselves.

And at this point we will ask: What are the things that we should ask the government to do for us which we cannot do for ourselves? The answer is: NOTHING. Government has neither a mystic nor a magic power. It is simply a collective, a socialized group of men seeking equality, which is impossible, and endeavoring to control individuals which is also impossible.

The dedicated individualist will examine himself and seek to control himself, fully. He will endeavor to weed out of his consciousness any feeling of defeatism, for it is defeatism which causes him to turn to the government for help.

Turning Away from Socialism

In other words, the dedicated individualist will be one who will turn away from government at every opportunity. He will not participate in political action. He will not attend mass meetings in an effort to elect some candidate. He will not write letters to his Congressman. He will not beseech the government, either for aid or for an end to aid. Each time he turns to government, even for a conservative desire, the government grows larger under the pleasure of his attention.

The individualist will not listen to government officials speaking on radio, on television, nor read about these speeches in newspapers. He will busy himself with enterprise and concentrate upon his own business, profession, vocation and avocation. Most of all, he will endeavor to weed out traces of collectivism, socialism, dependency and similar shortcomings from his own character.

Of course, the individualist knows that he cannot completely ignore government, even if he would. The government has the guns and will come upon him for tribute. The individualist will not imagine that he can lie or cheat his way out from under government domination. He will surrender to the government when he has to surrender. But he will not surrender beforehand. He will, in every sense of the word known to him, be an individualist and not a socialist.

Perhaps the best advice to individualists who wish to oppose the onward march of socialism under the guns of the government, is to be found in Ayn Rand's great book, "Atlas Shrugged." Although this work is in novel form, and consequently is frequently spurned by serious students of liberty, it is possible that it may play a decisive part in the struggle against socialism. Miss Rand causes one of her leading characters to utter this telling statement, on page 479:

". . . I choose to be consistent and I will obey you in the manner that you demand. Whatever you wish me to do, I will do it at the point of a gun. If you sentence me to jail, you will have to send armed men to carry me there — I will not volunteer to move. If you fine me, you will have to seize my property to collect the fine — I will not volunteer to pay it. If you believe that you have the right to force me — use your guns openly. I will not help you to disguise the nature of your action."

The practical results of this type of resistance to government coercion should be readily discernible. First of all, so far as the individual is concerned, it should mean a burst of new energy available to him for his own endeavor, whatever it is. If he minds his own business and avoids all political and governmental activity of any kind or description within his power, he should go far. Nor should he wait to take this step for himself until he has assured himself that others, too, plan to take it. The true individualist does not concern himself with the affairs of others.

But as the doctrine of individualism grows — as it must grow if the hydra of socialism is to be defeated — the governmentalists will discover a strange phenomenon developing. Fewer and fewer people will interest themselves in political activity. Instead of an increase in letter writing to politicians, there will be a decrease. Thus, there will be reason to let go administrative assistants who will finally have nothing to do.

Instead of having more and more people voting on more and more issues, there will be fewer and fewer people voting, and, consequently, fewer issues. This is the only way, without a violent revolution, for the tide of socialism to be halted. And there is no assurance that a violent revolution, even if successful, would halt the tide. In other words, the roots of socialism must be burned out. And the roots of socialism are in YOU.

Compulsion or Cooperation

Let us look at it this way for a moment. There are two great agencies in which men have learned to pool their energies for the accomplishment of major undertakings. These two agencies are: 1) government; 2) market place.

All use of force comes from the government; all production, from the market place.

Let us assume a society consisting of 100 persons, each of whom has ten units of energy. If 100 persons were free to produce, and if no force was exerted to prevent them from producing, this society could produce 1000 units of production.

This would be a society which would be using its maximum productive energy. Such a society would be producing at 100 percent of capacity.

Let us now suppose the opposite. We will imagine a society consisting of the same number of persons, each of whom has ten units of energy. But this society will put all of its energy into government. It will concentrate on using force.

How much production will occur in this society? The answer is zero production. However noble the members of this 100 percent governmental community might feel, they would all quickly starve to death. Men cannot live without production. They can live very well without force.

Now we get to the practical aspects of the matter. Production is the important factor. Our concern is to find ways and means of coming as close as possible to 100 percent productivity. Anything less than 100 percent is a risk which lessens our chances both of survival and of civilization.

Let us suppose this same society of 100 has 500 units of energy devoted to government and 500 devoted to production. The units of energy devoted to government would be parasitical in nature. They would consume only. The only thing they could consume would be the production provided by the other 500 units.

This society would destroy itself, though not as rapidly as the 100 percent governmental society. There would not be enough production to keep both producers and government personnel alive.

Survival becomes possible only in those societies where something more than 50 percent of all available energy is devoted to production. Thus, government must be reduced in size to less than 50 percent of the total amount of energy available.

The point is made by Lewis C. Ord in his book, "Politics and Poverty" (Mayflower Publishing Company, Ltd., London — 1948). He is contrasting the Russian system, which relies so firmly upon government energy, with other systems not so relying.

"Ultimately Russia would have been as completely equipped with the tools of industrial production as any other nation. When this had been accomplished in full, the failure of the great experiment could not have been concealed. As well equipped as any other nation, using large quantities and standardization in greater degree than anyone else, all industries nationalized, using scientific management and planning by the state to their maximum extent, the workers of Russia would nevertheless have remained poorer than the workers of any other great industrial nation. That would have been the final, the inevitable result.

"That their efforts failed, is not the fault of the Russians. The bureaucracy that is government in Russia absorbs vast numbers. The bureaucracy they have made of industry absorbs more. Their security police requires immense numbers. Their fighting forces require many more. With all these calls on man and woman power, the percentage of the total population in Russia left to do productive work is relatively small. It is the shortage of people left to do productive work that keeps the workers in Russia poor today. The same situation has developed to a less degree in other countries of Europe."

The same situation now confronted the western world including America. If it intinges upon our 100-unit society, the same result will manifest.

The margin of profit in a competitive market is so small, the dependence of productive expansion upon that narrow margin so great, I would like to hazard a guess that if more than five percent of a given society devote themselves to government, that society will begin to move down grade. Rather than stating such a conclusion categorically, I am going to say this. A primitive society, having a simple economy and using only a small amount of specialization, can afford to carry a fairly large bureaucratic overhead. While it is true that most primitive communities carry a small bureaucracy, there is such enormous waste of time, so much waste of energy in superstitious observation, witchcraft, games, dances and the like, only a relatively small portion of the society's energy is ever expended in productive effort.

When a society begins to advance, when specialization occurs and tools improve, the amount of wasted energy which is permissable begins to diminish. I submit that the more advanced the social structure, the less that structure can manage to survive the loss of energies misdirected into governmental channels. When large amounts of available energy are so directed, the society will begin to retrogress to a point equivalent to its more primitive forebears.

A highly evolved social structure can only come about through the diminution of governmental energy. The highest and most perfect form would occur at that point where productive energies achieved the 100 percent mark, and the governmental energies to be wasted reached zero.

CHAPTER 13

ONCE UPON A TIME

We can find no better means for exploring politics than by examining briefly and with some penetration the history of the origin of these United States. Perhaps there is no better way to assist one in making a penetrating self-analysis. Most of us are intimately acquainted with life in these United States. It would be instructive for us to learn just how and when these ideas became paramount in the general opinion:

1. The individual must surrender his personal liberty so that "society" will be free.

2. The voice of the majority is the voice of God.

3. Any kind of political maneuvering is justified because the ends are far more important than any means for accomplishing the ends.

In a prior chapter, the advantages accruing from life in these United States during our free enterprise years have already been shown. Many believe that the cause of the progress and development of free Americans is the extension of suffrage which gives every citizen the opportunity to express himself at the polls. Whether or not this is true, let us begin by an examination into the background of the people of the original colonies in this nation.

Socialist Antecedents

The settlers who came to these shores came from nations which were already largely socialized. In England, France, Germany, Holland, and other spawning grounds of our colonists, such extensive regulation of the means of production and distribution had already occurred that men did not believe that opportunities existed for them in their native lands. They migrated to America, knowing that America had to abound in opportunity since here there was little government to be reckoned with.

To a large degree it can be demonstrated that the waves of immigration to these shores were shifts of population impelled by European socialism. Of course, before Marx advertised socialism, few thought of the process as socialistic. They thought of it rather as a system of privilege in which the ruling nobility had all the advantages and taxed the producers of wealth into a state of perpetual poverty.

However we wish to term the theories under which the then civilized world operated, the fact is that socialism was the keynote, with a special order of highwaymen installed in offices of power. It was to escape these highwaymen that our forefathers fled to these shores.

They well know that there was no security for them here. Rather, they faced a well-publicized frontier of boundless opportunities, boundless freedom, and few if any other advantages. A minority fancied that they could get rich quick on these alien shores and then return to the old country to enjoy their profits. By far the majority came here to set up homes and to live a new life free from the exactions and cruelties imposed upon them by a controlled and regulated economy.

So vast was the distance which separated the colonists from the thrones of their respective monarchs, that for all practical purposes the motley horde that descended upon the Atlantic seaboard was ungoverned. The fact was particularly striking in the freest and most productive colonies.

True, there were numerous colonial satrapies established. But the governor of each colony, holding a franchise from his king which permitted him to collect taxes, control imposts, levy tariffs and the like, was so far removed geographically from the seat of enforcement that in a large measure the colonists, particularly the British colonists, did as they pleased.

The Spanish and French kings who established settlements are deserving of recognition for their attempt to create in the new world an extension of the old world slave society. The colonists were like little children, to begin with, eager to please their kings, delighted to do as they were told. But whenever this charming submission came up against the facts of existence as it is, the colonial governors found themselves unable to enforce the simplest edict. The frontiers were so large and so near. The target of legal action could and did take to the hills or woods, and government, insofar as enforcement was concerned, rested largely on the willing acquiescence of the people, or it existed not at all.

Planned Welfare

We know of no writing so descriptive of the times as that of Rose Wilder Lane in her book, "Discovery of Freedom."

"Eager to build settlements in New France and New Spain, the French and Spanish kings gave the land, in communal fields, to selected peasants of good character, sound morals, and industrious habits. The governments gave them carefully detailed instructions for clearing and fencing the land, caring for the fence and the gate, and plowing and planting, cultivating, harvesting, and dividing the crops.

"The government allotted land for the village, to be built as in Europe, a compact mass of cottages. It protected the villages by a detachment of soldiers, and a well-built fort.

"In every settlement, a commandant kept order and dispensed justice, usually with much human sympathy and wisdom. Typically, he addressed the settlers as 'my children' and they were obedient, well cared for, and gay. They had no trouble with the Indians. They learned the Indians' ball games, and played ball, raced horses, fought cocks, feasted and danced and sang, and gambled a great deal. They enjoyed safety, leisure, and enough to eat, in the American wilderness.

"During a century, the kings of France established such snug little settlements from the Atlantic along the St. Lawrence, around the Great Lakes, down the Mississippi Valley to Mobile and New Orleans. Before Thomas Jefferson was born, there was a little Versailles in Illinois; ladies and gentlemen in silks and satins and jewels were riding in sedan chairs to the Twelfth Night balls, and Indians and happy villagers, fatter than any in Europe, crowded outside the ballroom to watch the gaiety.

"The English kings were never so efficient. They gave the land to traders (Pennsylvania and Georgia, of course, were later given to philanthropists). A few gentlemen, who had political pull enough to get a grant, organized a trading company; their agents collected a ship-load or two of settlers and made an agreement with them which was usually broken on both sides.

"Landed in America, the colonists were never sure of getting the promised supplies; if the company's directors did not send them, the colonists died. But the directors could not depend on the settlers; they didn't work, they didn't get the expected furs, and the bound servants, especially, were always skipping out to live with the Indians.

"When Raleigh's promised supplies did not arrive, his whole colony vanished, and today you can talk with men from the Carolina foothills to the Osage mountains in Oklahoma who swear that their ancestors were in Raleigh's 'lost colony,' and that they simply moved to the mainland and up into the mountains.

"To the scandalized French, the people in the English colonies seemed liked undisciplined children, wild, rude, wretched subjects of bad rulers. Their villages were unplanned, their houses were scattered, they did not cultivate the land in common (though the towns did have communal pastures); their harvests were not equally divided, and they were always quarreling with each other and with the Indians. Their settlements split into factions; rebels left them and made other settlements. From the Great Lakes to the Gulf, in 1750, 'Bostonian' meant what 'Bolshevik' meant in this country twenty years ago.

"These unmanaged settlements all grew much more rapidly than the French and Spanish settlements. They grew so rapidly that in a hundred and fifty years they numbered more than a million persons, and the rate of population-growth was rapidly increasing. . . ."

And here was the point. The English colonies were unplanned, free and open to the individualistic nature of the inhabitants. They were rebellious of authority. The French and

Spanish colonies were planned, controlled and safe. But there was no room for individualistic developments. Consequently, when an English colonist wished to accomplish some particular chore he did so, probably right in the colony where he resided. And the king's representative could like it or not as he chose. But in a French or Spanish colony, the individualist wishing to depart from the controlled and regimented atmosphere had to depart physically. So he pulled up stakes and headed into the wilderness.

The vigor of expansion occurred in those colonies in which a minimum of regimentation resided. Elsewhere, little or no growth developed.

We can trace the predominance of British influence in this country to the freedom of its settlers. Had the French or Spanish kings relaxed their vigilance over their "children" it is possible that today we would be speaking and writing either French or Spanish rather than English. After all, the French and the Spanish had the advantage in most places of prior settlement and prior claim.

But the early American, throwing out his chest and breathing deeply the atmosphere of liberty, became in a few generations a rugged and independent human being. He was self-reliant because he had to be. He owned no man to be his better. He soon learned to kneel to none but God and even to keep his hat on in the presence of the king's representatives.

His eyes sought the verdure of the ever-present forest. The mists of spring and autumn kissed the hills ever at hand. Strange new ideas of human rights began to fill his mind. When he decided to open a forge, establish a mill, grow wheat, shoot quail, trap beaver, get married, raise a family, break horses, mine gold, hire out as a carpenter, make bricks, go to sea, become a merchant or a drummer, he did so. If the king's representative didn't like it, the cocky upstart thumbed his nose at vested authority and moved to a new location, or he stayed where he was and did as he pleased.

When taxes oppressed him, he refused to pay them. When the king brought in regiments to collect them, he tarred and feathered the tax collectors. He drank strong ale and stronger wine, he uttered seditious and treasonous speech with great glee, he worshipped where he would and even was so bold as to stay away from the state-supported church; and whenever he sniffed out any type of oppression leveled against him or his, he fought back with vigor, or he ignored it, or he moved away.

For nearly 150 years BEFORE the Declaration of Independence was written, the men and women of America were giving indication they knew freedom meant the absence of restraining force. And during those years, a series of indolent and passive rulers on the throne of England enhanced their spiritual and moral outlook by doing nothing for them.

Thus it happened when the third German George (III) grasped the British scepter of dominion and swore he would be a progressive and an industrious king, the colonists were steeped in seven generations of being let alone. So far as they were concerned, the alleged "divine right" of the British monarch to collect taxes from them was foolish.

George might be able to regulate and govern trade in the British Isles. All the more reason for him to leave the settlers alone. When it became apparent he wasn't going to leave them alone, a few spirited colonists like Tom Paine, Tom Jefferson, the Adams boys, George Mason and others formulated a doctrine which proved that a monarch who inherits political power has no divine right to rule. They made an intellectual travesty of monarchy which shook the foundations under every throne in the world.

High Treason

This was treason, as the members of the Virginia house of burgesses tried to warn Patrick Henry. He would not heed their warning! He counselled that the next breeze from the north might bring with it the sound of clashing arms. And as far as he was concerned, he would have liberty . . . liberty from the clutches of a divinely appointed sire . . . or he would take death!

The timid trembled. But the time had come. The death knell to a PARTICULAR TYPE of tyrannous rule had been sounded in these colonies. The farmers, merchants, drummers, hunters, trappers, fishermen and seamen sprang to arms. Who was the leader?

Here is the curious central fact of the American rebellion against monarchy. There was no leader. This was true because there was no government in the normal meaning of the word. For seven score years and more the Americans had scorned the time-honored political concepts of the old world. Sam Adams started the Committees of Correspondence. Information of the latest misdeeds of the king and the king's men was passed from colony to colony and into the far reaches of the frontier.

The "Sons of Liberty," consisting in the main of hot-headed youth, the "hot-rod" set of their day, banded together to give the king's expensively dressed regulars a hard time. Each colony had its spokesman; each community, its savant counselling freedom from oppression.

Against the wishes of the king, the Articles of Confederation were drawn up. There was little leadership and what there was vacillated to and from with each dispatch. George Washington, an ardent Tory, took a trip on horseback and someone thrust a copy of Tom Paine's mighty "Common Sense" into his hands. He read it and was convinced separation of the colonies from the mother country had to come.

The sedition spread. On every hand there were those who advocated an outright break. But on every hand were those who advocated submission and a patient subservience. The land was seething in political ferment. Gradually, a pattern of resistance to political oppression took form.

A gang of exuberant Bostonians turned the waters of Boston harbor into a tea cozy. Another gang, mostly from Rhode Island, rowed out into the bay and captured an armed gun boat flying His Majesty's colors and which, at the moment, was attempting to capture one of John Hancock's merchant ships laden with contraband. Hancock was a black market operator and smuggler. The men in the rowboat swarmed aboard the Gaspee, beat up the captain and crew, and burned the ship to the water's edge.

The Minute Men were organized. They VOLUNTEERED to stop whatever they were doing at a minute's notice to stand off further incursions from the British crown.

Came the dawn of April 19, 1775. A thin, reedy line of fewer than 100 Minute Men met at Buckley's tavern on the Boston corner of Lexington's green. The hale and hearty tavern keeper, routed out at 3:00 A.M., plied each man with a mug of something called rum flip. The ingredients are secret to this day, but the mugs were enormous.

Those untrained, bleary-eyed farmers formed a line across the common. "Stand your ground. Don't fire unless fired upon. But if they mean to have a war, let it begin here."

Remember the words? And remember, no government told Captain John Parker, another volunteer, to utter them.

Here was a declaration of independence backed up by outright rebellion almost a year and a half BEFORE the historically credited leaders of the rebellion got around to putting it on paper.

The British troops under the orders of General Gage had little trouble in dispersing the rebels. They marched on to Concord, the objective of their foray. They were supposed to arrest Sam Adams and John Hancock. But both men had been warned and were nowhere to be found. The ammunition and supplies gathered there, a secondary aim of the expedition, had been spirited away before the troops arrived. Empty-handed, they retraced their steps to Boston.

But now the countryside was aroused. Now the patriots, loving freedom more than they loved their political system, got behind fences, walls, trees and buildings. The march to Boston was increased to quick time, then to double time. The march became a retreat. Then a rout.

The countryside was alive. Each man shot what and when he pleased. No man led the opposition. The only official leader on both sides was the British officer in charge. And he was so busy trying to dodge those singing pellets that he had no time to try to seek the leaders of the rebellion. To this day, no one is certain. Everyone was responsible for his own actions that day.

The men who answered liberty's call took their positions because they would rather do it than not do it. Any man who didn't want to get out of his nice, warm bed on that frosty morning stayed put. But the ones who did get up earned an everlasting debt of gratitude from all who benefited by the freedom they voluntarily won on that day.

What Came Naturally

Follow the course of the revolutionary war if you will. It is a record of free men doing what came naturally to them — fighting for the right to be free of political dominance.

From Bunker Hill to Valley Forge, from New York to Yorktown, the Americans, backed finally by French allies, retreated. The revolt against the British crown could properly be called a retreat to victory. Half the time the Continental Congress was in flight. Most of the time there was no money to pay the troops. Forever the troops were poorly armed and equipped.

But there was no draft. There was no compulsion. Rarely did Washington, who finally accepted the overall command, know who was in his army. Men came and went. There was sickness, privation and hardship — and an indomitable spirit.

And here is an important point. This war was not fought so the Constitution could be written. On the contrary, the war was fought before the Constitution was even a dream. The battle of Yorktown, which ended the hostilities, occurred in 1781. The call for the Constitutional Convention which drafted and then urged the adoption of a Constitution didn't go out until September 17, 1787. It took six years before even a few of the colonists could convince themselves that a major central government was needed. Having just experienced the pain and anguish of breaking off the yoke of one kind of tyrant, they did not desire a second yoke.

We come now to a most sensitive point. Historian Charles Beard, in his book, "An Economic Interpretation of the Constitution of the United States," (published in 1913) dropped a bombshell, the fragmentations from which have been of aid and comfort to the socialists for at least two score years.

In this study, Beard maintained the Constitution was the deliberate work of a particular economic group. His charge was that the document was the offspring of the monied and propertied class and was set up deliberately to hold down the working classes and to exploit them, at the same time it protected and benefited those of superior economic position and advantage.

For a long time the charge went unanswered. There were few in this country who were willing to undertake the enormous research necessary to refute this allegation. Finally, in 1958, Forrest McDonald, working through the American History Research Center of Madison, Wisconsin, did so. His book, "We the People," (University of Chicago Press) is the most painstaking and thoroughly workmanlike job undertaken to refute Professor Beard.

But while Dr. McDonald lays the ghost of the Beard accusation, his study uncovers a wealth of political chicanery which accompanied the drafting and the ratification of the Constitution, albeit the maneuverings are shown to be devoid of primary economic motivation.

Economic Motivation

Those who opposed the ratification and adoption of the Constitution were, in many instances, as economically solvent as those who favored it. Clearly, in its antecedents, the Constitution was NOT the work of the monied classes. However, notwithstanding McDonald's exhaustive efforts it is still possible that those who favored and those who opposed the Constitution's adoption, took their positions for economic reasons.

It may be those men of means who favored the formation of a stronger central power believed their financial position would be enhanced thereby; and it is equally possible those who opposed the formation did so for an identical reason. Men are not gifted with prescience. And since Dr. McDonald was compelled to work backward from the known results of the Constitution, it is a little too extensive a stretch of our credulity to suppose that either 1) all of the men who contended on this issue were gifted with foresight or — 2) all of the men who thus contended were devoid of economic interests.

In any case, some men were aided financially by the adoption of the document and some men were not. (Nor were all of those aided, those who favored it; and those harmed, those who opposed.)

Before considering this important milestone in the history of government, it must be stressed that the Constitution as a document is not the truly important item to be considered. The Constitution was designed with the principle of men's independence and economic individuality in mind. What must now be asked is this. Has the Constitution proved to be the safeguard for individual free enterprise that our founders hoped it would be?

Has it stood the test of time? Has it retained its basic nature of providing for a limited government of dispersed power? Or, has it, rather, escaped the mold into which it was poured, and burgeoned outward until today it has become as oppressive as some prior and contemporary forms?

What is important is the true nature of man. If the Constitution has done the job outlined for it, namely, that of providing a centralized agency for the purpose of insuring all of men's basic rights in freedom, then we must be content with the Constitution.

If, on the other hand, we must "get back to the Constitution," proving thereby we are no longer protected by it, then we must be candid enough in our appraisal to recognize that it contained certain basic flaws. We must be willing to examine it carefully, not as though it were a divine instrument struck off by angels, but rather as though it were what it is, an instrument of government in keeping in some places with man's nature, and in violation in some places of man's nature, but in no way so holy and so sacrosanct that it must not be analyzed. Surely, a Constitution can be improved upon as well as degraded. Surely, we are not banned from cutting government down in size or even eventually abolishing all powers it has taken which it uses to invade human rights.

It is absurd to suggest that all we have to do is to adhere to a particular written Constitution if it can be shown that the particular form has already been breached by the clever manipulations of those who seek to convert America into an old-world despotism of either Platonic, Marxian or Fabian character.

If the Constitution can protect our basic rights, then let us stick with it. If it cannot, then let us not hamper ourselves with an ineffective tool. What is important is our basic rights. If what began as an instrument for protecting an individualistic economy has been altered so it has become an instrument for inducing a new kind of democratic tyranny, the quicker we wake up to the fact, the better.

We must take care at this juncture in American life that we do not lose the spirit of liberty in an adherence to a form which no longer contains the spirit. A bottle which has been emptied of the elixir it contained, should not be a subject of worship. It is simply an empty container. It is the elixir which must be preserved.

Under motivations the depth and extent of which we will probably never know, a group of sincere and dedicated veterans of the American conflict with Britain set themselves the task of providing a "more perfect union." Among these men were such stalwarts as Alexander Hamilton, John Jay and James Madison. But among the American colonists who opposed the adoption of the Constitution were such men as John Hancock, who helped pay for the revolution; Patrick Henry, whose inspiring speeches helped trigger the revolution; and George Mason, one of the outstanding libertarian minds of his generation.

As Professor McDonald reveals, the political footwork to secure ratification of the Constitution was engineered even while the delegates were battling over the nature of the instrument. Clearly, there was a strong and urgent desire in certain quarters to set up a federal government at whatever cost, regardless of what it provided.

"Thus, in the Convention, even as they debated principles and haggled over details, they were writing into the Constitution the first provision in their future political strategy. This was Article VII, the process of ratification: *The ratification of the Conventions of nine States, shall be sufficient for the*

Establishment of this Constitution between the States so rati-fying the same. Harmless enough on its face, this provision stacked the deck in the forthcoming contest and virtually assured ratification."

By holding special conventions in each state, rather than relying upon the existing state legislatures, those favoring ratification employed an astute device enabling them to pack delegates into these special conventions which process was barred them had they depended upon the normal representation. Additionally, by creating a situation in which the ratification of nine states would automatically validate the Constitution, an instrument of pressure was created which tended to whip the remaining four states into line. A combine of nine states would be too strong for four separate sovereign states to oppose.

Here is Professor McDonald again:

"This seventh article, together with the complementary resolutions sent to Congress and to the several states, reveals the nature of the contest, at least in the minds of Federal strategists . . . It was STATES as such which had to be won, and the design of Article VII, and the strategy of the Federalists were geared to this fact."

The Constitution was not adopted by the people of the colonies in anything resembling a general election. Nor were their representatives, drawn together under the Articles of Confederation, permitted to vote on the issue. The political strategem was to by-pass both of these means and to place the issue squarely before a group of persons carefully drawn together for the especial purpose.

The plan to provide the colonies with a strong central government began to be noised about during the days following the revolutionary war in which a treaty of peace was being negotiated with Britain.

Political Strategy

The idea was slow to take hold. One of the staunchest opponents of the scheme was Thomas Jefferson, the bold author of the Declaration of Independence. At this time Jefferson was serving in the Confederate Congress. His comments against the adoption of a stronger central authority were so pertinent a move was undertaken to ship him to England to negotiate the treaty and thus to get him out of the way. He turned down the first proposal to this effect, but as treaty efforts continued to languish he finally agreed to go when the second offer was made.

Jefferson was strongly opposed to slavery, despite the fact he was himself a slave owner. He could see the single possible advantage to a strong central government as residing in a permanent decree against the practice. But this single advantage did not seem to him of sufficient importance to justify the formation of an entire federal government simply to obtain it. He was a strong exponent of states' rights and it was well known then, and is well known now, that his position was "that government is best which governs least."

His political faction was strong in Virginia, and Virginia was not only a key state insofar as the ultimate union was concerned, but contained the one man the Federalists wanted as president, George Washington, himself.

Jefferson had already served two terms as governor of Virginia, and when he absented himself to go to the Congress and afterwards to go abroad, Patrick Henry, another strong anti-Federalist, became governor.

By the time Jefferson's second appointment came, the treaty had been successfully concluded and his sailing was deferred. The Federalists were desperate. They dared not ignore Jefferson if they sent out a call for a Constitutional Convention. Yet, they feared his opposition. What to do? Someone got a brilliant idea and proposed it. Jefferson could be sent to France as an assistant to Benjamin Franklin, who had served and was serving brilliantly as minister. Jefferson, amenable finally to a sojourn on British soil, was successfully redirected to the courts in Paris. Although Franklin needed no assistance, the strong champion of states' rights went to France to provide it.

Now, the Federalists played a trump card. Franklin was an old man and politically open to a strong central government, albeit one with severe limitations. It would be better to have

Franklin in the States than Jefferson. Both men had reputations as statesmen. Both were dedicated to the cause of freedom. Either could be counted upon to lead his followers in whichever direction was finally taken.

In 1785 Jefferson took over Franklin's duties as minister to France and the aging author of "Poor Richard" came back to America and was asked to serve as delegate to the convention, where he could lend dignity to the proceedings and, it was hoped, swing his followers into line behind the new government.

So Jefferson was not present at the Constitutional Convention and did not return to the States until the end of 1789, after the document had been ratified. He had nothing to do with its framing or approval. Later on, he was to support it stoutly.

Franklin and the Constitution

Let us examine Benjamin Franklin's conduct at the meeting in Philadelphia.

"Franklin, Apostle of Modern Times," by Bernard Fay, gives us some insight into the general thinking of the delegates at the convention and also a view as to Franklin's particular philosophy respecting government.

As to the delegates, Fay says: "They were directly opposed to Franklin's philosophical tendency, which might be summed up in this formula: the least government possible is the greatest possible good."

On page 504 of this biographical sketch, Mr. Fay describes what transpired during that hot and sultry summer in Philadelphia.

"Throughout the session of the Convention, Franklin advocated lost causes and praised French liberalism in which no one was interested. Three theories were particularly dear to him: the danger of paying government officials high salaries; the necessity of establishing a feeble, plural executive body; and the justice of representation which was proportioned to the population and the State's wealth.

"He was beaten on all three points. In spite of his speech on June 2, liberal salaries were attached to all federal appointments; in spite of his address on June 11, which urged that the smaller states accept equal taxation if they demanded equal representation, the smaller States won out. He had to propose a compromise himself, to the effect that the equal representation should be maintained except on financial measures. But this was not enough; the Convention agreed to establish a federal Senate; to which each State would send an equal number of representatives. Franklin had no success, either, in his proposition for a multiple executive body (June 30).

"The Convention did not talk the same language as he did. On June 28 after hours of vain discussion in this question of representation, Franklin suggested they have recourse to prayer and ask heaven for assistance. His discourse, which was brief but moving, and filled with Biblical piety, would have made the ladies of Passy weep, but it had no effect whatsoever on the American delegates. One of them answered with a crushing objection: the Convention did not have the money to pay for a minister! There was a short discussion and Franklin was forced to realize that 'the convention, except three or four persons, thought prayers unnecessary' . . ."

His final speech is excerpted for us by the biographer.

"I confess that I do not entirely approve of this Constitution, at present . . . In these sentiments, Sir, I agree to this Constitution, with all its faults, — if they are such; because I think a general government necessary for us and there is no *form* of government but what may be a blessing to the people, if well administered; and I believe, further, that this is likely to be well administered for a course of years and can only end in despotism, as other forms have done before it, when the people shall become so corrupted as to need despotic government, being incapable of any other."

Fay sums it up as follows:

"Thanks to this speech, the plan of the Convention was adopted unanimously and became the Constitution of the United States. From the standpoint of public opinion, his intervention was decisive, for the people were rather hostile to this new project, and would have probably rejected it if a leader such as Franklin had denounced it. Thus, he had played an important role at the Convention but it was political suicide; he had helped to organize a regime which was different from what he wanted, from what he had been recommending for thirty years, and he had put a group of men in power who had no confidence in him."

Thus Franklin played the Federalists' tune and Jefferson was out of the way. What of Samuel and John Adams, stalwart backers of the revolution?

Adams and Hancock

Privately, Sam Adams had expressed himself as having strong reservations against the Constitution. He would not serve as delegate. But he would make no public statement either pro or con. John took a similar position. To secure the backing of the Adamses was an important and necessary step in the process of ratification. Massachusetts was a vital state. And the Adamses were cold to the proposal while John Hancock, also from Massachusetts, was openly hostile.

So the Federalists held a mass meeting at the famed Old Green Dragon Inn two days before the Constitutional convention was held. Some 400 participants, mechanics and tradesmen of Boston rallied to the cause of the Federalists and the Adams boys were witness to the drama. Seeing what appeared to be large public sentiment in favor of the Constitution, Sam announced that he would support ratification.

Hancock was another story. But the Federalists were competent to deal with him. According to Dr. McDonald, "To enlist Hancock's support the Federalists promised to support him for the vice presidency or, if Virginia did not ratify in time to qualify Washington, even for the presidency. Nothing could have appealed to Hancock more, and he gave his support to ratification."

Hancock, of course, was not the vice president finally selected by the Federalists.

The final major battle for ratification was to be fought out in Virginia.

Here, notwithstanding Washington, the absent Jefferson's influence was strong. And the esteem and prestige of Patrick Henry was so great the contest became virtually a personal campaign between Henry and Washington. Henry was eloquent. It is said by McDonald that at a single meeting where Henry spoke, he managed to convert three Federalist delegates to the anti-Federalist cause. He portrayed the destruction of human liberty under the Constitution in such vivid phrases that the witness "involuntarily felt his wrists to assure himself that the fetters were not already pressing his flesh."

For sheer political wizardy and compelling behind-the-scenes maneuvering, the adoption of the American Constitution has few parallels. The adoption came. And the course of history was set.

The heroic men and women who struggled to insure us an atmosphere of liberty were under pressures the like of which have only become parallel in modern times. Disunited, alone, facing a world of great potential hostility, it was only normal and natural for our forebears to band together. Of course, they had just defeated on the field of battle the most powerful empire in existence. But the cost of this effort had been enormous. The colonists were exhausted by the effort and could not have looked abroad without the fear that some other nation might swoop down upon them to find them weak and illy-prepared for future hostilities. If they moved to institute an agency of arbitrary and artificial might, one cannot blame them. Not the slightest breath of criticism for their fears and apprehensions is intended or implied. Provide again the unique situation with which our ancestors were faced and there would be few of us who would counsel a course of action other than the one finally taken.

While the colonists viewed a situation that was unique, so, too, do we, their descendants, face a unique period of history. And what we must do is to blaze a new trail, mark a new pathway into greater liberty, not be content merely to rest on past glory and presume that everything has already been accomplished.

Some men sincerely felt the cause of freedom would be aided by the Constitution. Others just as sincere, believed the cause of freedom would be harmed. It is not our purpose here to decry or to defame the splendid dedicated men who labored either for or against ratification of the document. It can be assumed each man had his motive, and we must assume these motives, however colored they may have been by each economic situation, were in the main altruistic and objective.

What is important for general realization is that many and brilliant were those who strongly opposed the instrument. Nor is their patriotism in question.

The Constitution was a human document which, so long as people were intent upon their own affairs, leaving government largely in other hands, served well enough. But, as time passed, efforts were made to convince the American people their progress, their industry, their productivity, were not the product of their own energies but, peculiarly, the product of their own government.

The government became, in the minds of many, great in itself and not merely fortunate by virtue of its limited and divided characteristics.

When the American people began to believe all of their good fortune flowed from the federal capital, it was natural for them to turn to that capital for the satisfaction of every known want and desire. Though government can never serve as an all-knowing and all-seeing father, there were political opportunists on hand to profit by the assumption.

This trend, which has developed slowly but steadily since the first days of ratification, has now reached alarming proportions. The reason for the alarm is the federal government is an artificial agency of might, unnatural and contrary to the desires and talents of a great host of American people. It will remain for present or future generations to decide whether or not the Constitution must be preserved at all costs, or whether individual liberty, personal privacy, initiative, self-reliance and responsibility in an environment of freedom are more productive of good for everyone.

While Communists may chant that they wish the Constitution abolished, Fabians and other Socialists are quite content with it. By modern interpretations of the meaning and purpose of the Constitution, the instrument is now serving to protect and sustain ideas which are hostile to personal freedom and independence.

Instead of protecting the free enterpriser from theft and incursions of various sorts, the federal government has become the largest single predator with which he must cope. The Constitution, as Franklin predicted, has become a device for furthering despotism. The bulwark designed to protect our freedom has been breached.

Not Far Enough

The leaders of the war against England didn't go far enough. Their conceptions were developed within the framework of their own time and place. They saw the necessity of limiting the power of government. Being intimately acquainted with the tyranny of the monarchial form, they were alert against it. In this, they were successful. There has been no sustained movement in these United States to establish a monarchy, although a few persons will, on occasion, venture that we should have a "strong man" government in order to put down persons and ideas of which they do not approve.

Additionally, our founding fathers saw that political power placed in the hands of the people can lead to disaster. They tried to devise a middle way, in which all power would be diffused, each unit of power serving to check some other unit of power so tyranny would be difficult. Where they effectively checked the amassment of power, the government did not function at all. Where the check was insufficient, the government functioned and grew.

According to Catherine Drinker Bowen in her book, "John Adams and the American Revolution," it was the consensus of opinion in those days that state governments must be instituted at once. Without these governments, two and a half million people could not conduct a continental war.

"Ever since June of 1775, when Massachusetts petitioned Congress to institute the first independent provisional government, John had urged the necessity of separate state constitutions. 'From the beginning,' John wrote later, 'I always expected we should have more danger and difficulty from our attempts to govern ourselves than from all the fleets and armies of Europe.'

"Everywhere, Royal Governors were on the run. Lord Dunmore had been chased out of Norfolk, Virginia and lived on a warship, where he complained he was 'reduced to the deplorable and disgraceful state of being a tame spectator of rebellion.' In New Jersey, Governor William Franklin, Dr. Franklin's illegitimate son, was arrested and put under guard by the patriots. Maryland's Governor Eden, a tactful gentleman, much liked, was allowed to remain at large. It was gratifying to be rid of these crown officers, yet their going left no government at all. Even the conciliation men admitted that some sort of provisional government must be constructed. They were careful to stress the word, provisional.

"The great question was, What form should these governments take? Thirteen colonies debated it. Interest was intense and penetrated to the remotest frontier households. If the war with Britain did not touch every cabin and settlement, the question of local government most certainly did touch them. They had absolutely nothing to go by; nowhere in Europe had popular government been tried on so large a scale. People were fearful of the unknown, the untried; each man looked to his own particular interest. Landowning patriots in New York and the Carolinas, with thousands of acres under their personal control, were naturally inclined toward a government by the aristocracy, which meant themselves. New England, on the other hand, inhabited by small traders and farmers, fishermen, storekeepers, desired governments far more democratical. Colonies, counties, towns sent in their stated preferences, 'that it is our opinion that we do not want any Governor but the Governor of the Universe, and under him a States General to consult with the rest of the States for the good of the whole'."

But while the leaders were doing their best to arrive at a type of government which would not govern; at a type of representation not completely representative; at a type of taxing authority that would not tax too severely, the people themselves followed their leaders but with less objectivity and less self-effacement.

The people rebelled against monarchy and the feudal concept of a divinely appointed nobility because they recognized that it gave a certain select few the opportunity to profit at the expense of others.

To begin with, they actually abolished government. It took two years before the state governments began to function feebly. In general, the people went on ignoring government. Sporadically, they resisted it here and there. Remember the "whiskey rebellion," the "interpositions" in Virginia and Kentucky, the resistance to tariffs in South Carolina's open ports? Then again there were the violent "anti-draft" riots in New York City which accounted for the lives of a thousand men in Civil War days. It was when the government began to dole out "free land" to the "poor" that the agency of authority began to be viewed as a giant cornucopia. The former rebels reached out for the magic word "republic." Later, they groped for the word "democracy" to justify their desire to get something for nothing. By believing in the efficacy of either or both of these words, they came to believe that they could join in with the "nobility" which they had rebelled against, and thus be nobles themselves by sharing in the profits others earn.

The cruel disillusionment with which we are dealing follows when it is realized that there are no "others." The system is cannibalistic and results in a condition in which all men employ the government to prey upon all other men.

Stripped of its attempted moral justifications, this is socialism.

Spirit of Liberty

The question for our generation and those following is this: Can we rediscover the spirit of liberty despite the Constitution, or must we forever be subjected to a *form* of government which has, in fine, protected liberty little better than previous forms?

Because of the initial thrust of liberty's clean blade, our country has forged ahead, and in contrast to the tyranny and capriciousness of other governments our political instrument has seemed superior. But when we turn our eyes once more towards liberty, we can realize how far we have drifted from the basic American fact, how inferior is the instrumentality which was designed to protect liberty, how vast is the difference between what we have and what our founders sought to attain.

Americans may fancy they have had freedom during the days since 1789 because of the Constitution. The fact is they had freedom notwithstanding the Constitution. Although the government we have had has been of assistance to punish wrong-doers, to maintain a large area of free trade and to wage warfare (if wars be useful), it has not been demonstrated that these services could not have been performed WHEN NECESSARY by other means.

It would take a volume larger than this to list and describe the instances in which our government, sometimes in contradiction of the Constitution and sometimes in accord with it, violated the *principles* of nature and of nature's laws.

A single example should suffice to show the fact of these violations was known and understood before our day by men of principle.

William Lloyd Garrison, at a fourth of July meeting of the Anti-Slavery Society in Framingham Grove near Boston, read the Fugitive Slave Act, and then read the court order of a federal judge handing a fugitive slave back to its owner. Having read them he set a match to both documents, crying as they burned, "And let all the people say Amen!"

Then Garrison raised high a copy of the Constitution of the United States, read its clauses that sanctioned slave property and declared the Constitution was the source of all other atrocities, terming it the "covenant with death and agreement with hell." Then, he burned the Constitution. Today, were someone to do this he would be called a Communist.

But Garrison was no Communist. Nor are the people Communists who object to communism or socialism as it is rammed down their throats today by means of legal forms.

From its earliest days of taxation, its conduct respecting slavery and the tariff, its broken treaties with Indians, its religious persecution of the Mormons, its harassment of various individuals, its bayonet-bearing paratroopers in Little Rock, its first illegal income tax under Abraham Lincoln, its first recourse to a compulsive draft which brought on a riot in New York City in which 1,000 innocent persons were killed, its employment of subsidies to bolster losing businesses at the expense of successful businesses, its aid to foreign despots, its debauchment of the currency, and its everlasting growth — all of these things should cause honest men to look at their government and inquire if this is the best that can be done. The bill of grievances contained in the immortal Declaration of Independence could be extended by our own citizens in modern times, had they the stomach for it.

Though some foreign agitators oppose the Constitution, their opposition is invariably calculated to legalize a stronger and more tyrannical power in Washington. As Americans and human beings, we should favor the principles of liberty, of independence, of private ownership, irrespective of documents.

The Declaration of Independence upon which the Constitution is based, and which is the primary legal instrument of this nation, contains these three sentences:

"That whenever any Form of Government becomes destructive of these ends, it is the Right of the People to alter or abolish it, and to institute new Government, laying its foundation on such principles and organizing its powers in such form, as to them shall seem most likely to effect their Safety and Happiness. Prudence, indeed, will dictate that Governments long established should not be changed for light and transient causes; and accordingly all experience hath shown, that mankind are more disposed to suffer, while evils are sufferable, than to right themselves by abolishing the forms to which they are accustomed. *But, when a long train of abuses and usurpations, pursuing invariably the same Object evinces a design to reduce them under absolute Despotism, it is their right, it is their duty, to throw off such Government, and to provide new Guards for their future security."*

So important is the right and the duty of the people to dispense with despotism, this great Declaration contains the sentence not once, but twice. In its final utterance, the choice of words does not call for the formation of a government. Rather, it calls for "new guards" which may or may not entail such a unit as an artificial government agency.

CHAPTER 14

BIRTH OF A MAN

It is time for the descendants of the early American patriots who fought and died for that poorly defined but magnificent idea, LIBERTY, to let their voices be heard once more. It is time for those newly arrived Americans, fleeing the atrocities and tyrannies of Europe and Asia, to speak up boldly in favor of the liberty they came here to find.

Humanity the world over is sunk under a weight of excessive bureaucracy sired by the socialist ideologists.

The American government is no more worthy in its present formation and policy to raise a banner of freedom than is the thundering crew of political slavemasters headquartered in the Kremlin.

Welding the Crack

If the crack in the liberty bell is to be welded shut so that the tocsin call to freedom can be heard among the world's oppressed, it must be free men OUTSIDE OF GOVERNMENT who perform this welding task. No government that curtails or inhibits individual liberty can possibly man the universal carillon.

What is needed is a rebirth of the spirit of liberty. The Declaration of Independence contained that spirit. But it was limited, not by the desire of the authors but by the circumstances under which it was produced. The oppressed colonists of that prior day were concerned with INDEPENDENCE FROM BRITAIN. The oppressed individualists of our generation are concerned with INDEPENDENCE FROM GOVERNMENT.

They are conscious that moral law must provide the base of their society. They are becoming conscious now that governments, by their very nature, tend to subvert moral law in the interests of expedience.

A new Declaration of Independence is in order. To meet the challenge of collectivism it must be a Declaration of **Individual** Independence.

The Declaration of Individualism

When, in the course of human events, it becomes necessary for ONE INDIVIDUAL to dissolve the political bands which have held him under the dominance of any state, and thus to assume his full stature as a human being among the others of his kind, in compliance with highest moral law and in conformity with nature's laws and in deep humility before nature's God, a decent respect to the opinions of mankind requires that he should declare the causes which impel him to thus stand forth a free being and subservient to none.

These truths are held to be self-evident, that each man is better qualified to govern his own affairs than any other man or combination of men or agencies are so qualified; that he is endowed by his Creator with certain unalienable rights, that among these are life, liberty, private ownership of property, and the pursuit of happiness. That to secure these rights, each man is qualified to select for himself that agency or those agencies which seem to him best suited to protect his life and his property, to maintain his freedom, and which lie within his ability to afford. That whenever any agency evinces characteristics of tyranny, he is well within his rights and his powers to discharge that agency and to find another more suitable to his inclinations and his finances. That he is competent to accomplish this end singly or jointly with others, with the express understanding that no single person may be coerced or trespassed against in the formation or the maintenance of any such joint enterprise.

Experience, indeed, will dictate that governments in practice erode and destroy the individuality of man by virtue of the coercion they exercise against their citizens. Therefore, he will take due cognizance of this fact, and should a new government be deemed advisable and most likely to effect his safety and happiness, he will see to it that the just powers of that government shall be derived from the INDIVIDUAL consent of those governed. No man shall be compelled to pay a tax for a product or service he does not wish to enjoy. On the contrary, each man wishing such product or service shall bear the full pro-rata cost of that product or service without resort to taxation.

No man, in making this INDIVIDUAL declaration, is seeking by so doing to overthrow or subvert any existing government. He is, rather, intent upon stopping the long train of abuses and usurpations which have pursued a single object of placing him under absolute despotism. If others want tyranny he is content to let them pursue it to their pleasure. He seeks only to stand free of the political shackles that fetter his own wrists.

He will not use force to secure his objective. He will obey the edicts of his rulers when he is compelled to obey. But he will no longer volunteer to further tyranny, either by beseeching subsidy or support, or by accepting it should it be granted him. He will make his own way, for better or for worse, and hold himself accountable to his God for his success and his failure.

The history of the present governments the world over is a history of repeated injuries and usurpations against humankind, having in direct object the subjugation and the socialization of every human being.

To prove this, let facts be submitted in candor to mankind.

1. Governments, as presently formulated, have demonstrated their inability to deal with crime. Rather, in certain cases where criminals have been apprehended, the laws have been perverted in such fashion that the courts themselves have conspired to aid the felon. There is a rising tide of lawlessness and delinquency. Yet, where "tough" policies have been enacted, so obtuse and oppressive are the rulings that

innocent persons are made to suffer indignities and oppressions of the worst sort, whereas hardened criminals easily secure their freedom.

2. Governments, as presently formulated, have demonstrated repeatedly that they are simply the tools of various pressure groups. Principles have been abandoned, in favor of expediency. And in those places where such pressures have been put down, the citizens live in a state of virtual siege with the government itself providing pressures and exactions against them.

3. Governments, as presently formulated, have so magnified the task of passing laws that in many places the body of law already exceeds the lifetime of scholars for reading purposes. Yet the process continues and it is so prolific of results that thousands of new codes, rules, regulations, ordinances and manifestos are issued each moment, the result of which is to place every citizen under the baneful necessity of obeying what he knows not of, and of paying for "benefits" which will never accrue to him.

4. Governments, as presently formulated, maintain the fiction of representation. But they are no longer either representative or responsive to the wishes or even the anguish of the individual citizen. Though it has been widely accepted that the democratic form of government provides a government of the people, by the people, and for the people, it is now seen that as governments are presently arrayed they are organizations of the government, by the government and for the government.

5 Governments, as presently formulated, are forever on the search for bigness and power. The tiny and self-contained, largely self-government unit is no longer viable. By the process of merger, metropolitanizing, federalizing and worldizing, through the agencies of bureaus, committees, appointees, and by means of laws, passed legally or put into activity illegally by executive fiat, a vast usurpation has occurred and is occurring so that the rights of the individual are forever placed under a growing cloud of oppression. In the United States as an example, each citizen is at once required to obey a minimum of six governing bodies—school district, city, county,

state, nation and United Nations. Since the rules in each case are both costly and in conflict, a mounting confusion grows. The answer given is for a vast merger to occur, a homogenizing of all power with central authority drifting irrevocably toward the hands of a supreme dictator. The rights of the individual have been cancelled out in favor of the bigness and the power of a bureaucracy.

6. Governments, as presently formulated, have long since abandoned their historic function of keeping law and order. They have usurped a thousand prerogatives and are now advancing the socialist cause by seizing businesses, charitable organizations and educational institutions which they operate in the face of mounting financial ruin on every hand. The seizure begins as the confiscation of income and wealth from the citizens. It ends with the government itself competing in every walk of life with the taxpayer, who must not only make a profit to subsist but must pay for the waste and abuse of monopolistic and monolithic competition.

7. Governments, as presently formulated, are engaged in co-mixing the funds of their own constituents with the

funds of constituents of other governments. A universal policy of plundering the citizen has supplanted the policy of a frugal and accountable regime. Additionally, and against all decent usage and custom, governments are compelling citizens to work, attend school, and live in neighborhoods among people with whom they have little in common. Governments are legislating in the field of morals and have declared, if God has not made man equal to each other man, he shall be made equal by universal force and an end of sufferance.

8. Governments, as presently formulated, have undermined individual responsibility by providing financial rewards for mothers of children born out of wedlock, by paying subsidies to persons who are unemployed, by rewarding those who refuse to produce. With the unprecedented rise in population and the mammoth support of the indigent and impecunious, the governments are now imaging a bureau to control population and another to further the peopling of other planets of this solar system.

9. Governments, as presently formulated, have lost touch with the sense of justice and reason. They have become tools of union agitators and will suffer almost any abuse to an individual citizen provided that abuse occurs under union management. They have recently, in the United States, endeavored to reveal racketeering in certain unions which are momentarily out of governmental favor. But the principles of coercion and violence in every labor union still stand unchecked.

10. Governments, as presently formulated, have penalized the successful and rewarded the unsuccessful, in violation of natural law.

11. Governments, as presently formulated, have made a mockery of courts, by causing judges to be responsive to the whim of popular leaders. The courts in large measure now mirror the will of the chief executive and justice is banished to places outside of government.

12. Governments, as presently formulated, have made a universal draft and military service compulsory, in violation of the rights of free men.

13. Governments, as presently formulated, have ringed the businessman and producer with a wall of regulations, licenses, reports, taxations, and vexations beyond all reason, to the detriment of all.

14. Governments, as presently formulated, have manipulated the currency, debauched the medium of exchange and brought a wholesale inflation upon the world to the ruination of the people.

15. Governments, as presently formulated, have interfered with the right of a man to travel where he pleases.

16. Governments, as presently formulated, have plundered the citizens of vast treasure to establish enormous propaganda agencies which serve in the capacity of singing the self-praise of each government.

17. Governments, as presently formulated, have moved into the realm of psychology and have presumed to decide who is sane and who is not sane with arbitrary treatment prescribed for those the governments find to be suffering from an unwillingness to obey or to sanction their immoral actions.

18. Governments, as presently formulated, have cut off the trade of some persons with the trade of other persons.

19. Governments, as presently formulated, have permitted their citizens to be tried in courts beyond their own jurisdiction, despite the fact that these citizens are under their exclusive regulation and have paid taxes for the support of their own system of jurisprudence.

20. Governments, as presently formulated, have raised the taxes repeatedly, compelling those who object to the taxes to pay at the same rate as those who do not object. Additionally, some are compelled through a form of involuntary servitude to act for the government and to collect taxes from others against their own will and against the will of others. Nor are they recompensed for so doing.

21. Governments, as presently formulated, have created a debt so monstrous that it will take generations of future citizens to cope with it and despite the moral question as to whether an unborn child can be held responsible for debts incurred before his birth.

22. Governments, as presently formulated, have confiscated private property, often for light and whimsical reasons, paying for the property at a rate pleasing only to the government.

23. Governments, as presently formulated, have set up arbitrary restrictions on the use of private property, preventing individuals from the full enjoyment of what they own.

24. Governments, as presently formulated, have taken up arms against ordinary citizens, have bayoneted harmless persons in the streets, and have stood by in the midst of lawless insurrection, giving countenance and standing to riot and property damage.

25. Governments, as presently formulated, have stimulated their own citizens to prepare to take up arms against possible foreign aggressors, while at the same time encouraging these potential foes with entertainment, largesse and legal advantages and immunities.

26. Governments, as presently formulated, have created a vacuum in the minds of youths by indoctrinating them from

their tenderest years in government institutions, which operate on the theory that money can do everything and that what the government demands in the way of money is always morally justified.

In every stage of these oppressions, individual citizens have petitioned for redress, in the most humble terms. Their repeated petitions have been answered only by repeated injury. Any government whose character is thus marked by every act which may define a tyranny, is unfit to be either the ruler of or the protector of individuals.

Nor has the individual been wanting in his esteem and affection for individual political figures he may know and admire. Repeatedly, these political figures have been asked to right the wrongs being heaped upon their fellow citizens. Party support has been switched, encouragement has been given to well-meaning and outspoken politicians who promise a surcease of these manifold woes. But to no avail. It appears that the government office is now so large that it dominates the man, and that no man in power is large enough to dominate his office.

Appeal has been made to a sense of justice, a sense of fair play, a sense of economy. The men in government have been deaf alike to the voices calling for justice or even for a recognition of the fact that they, too, are human.

Therefore, while the necessity is deplored, it must be declared that men in office who are performing coercive functions in violation of nature's laws have become themselves a part of the state, which is the source of the difficulties. They are either helpless to right these numerous wrongs, or they are willingly perpetrating them.

I, therefore, a citizen of this nation, standing by myself and exerting no influence or coercion over any, and appealing to the Supreme Judge of the world for the rectitude of my intentions, do, in the name and by the authority which resides in all free men, solemnly publish and declare, that I am and of right ought to be a free and independent human being. I will therefore, now and henceforward, refrain from participation in all agencies of government whenever and wherever I am permitted. I will be independent and self-supporting, looking neither to government nor to any similar agency of force to provide for me. Nor will I willingly join with any organization, group, or person who counsels or urges violence, coercion, or the forceful regulation of my fellow man in any particular whatsoever.

And for the support of this Declaration, I pledge my life, my fortune and my sacred honor.

The idea and the ideal of individual resolve will be slow to take hold. Men are gregarious and by instinct fearful of full reliance on their independent judgment. But the case for individualism will rest its plea on the laws of nature and nature's God, and it will be justly judged in time.

There will always be those who will assure themselves they would like to be a full-fledged individualist if only they could be certain that others would take the same position. The true individualist will not permit himself to be comforted or protected by that alibi. The true individualist will root out all traces of socialism within himself and act independently, even though he may be the only person to so strip himself of comfort and to so act.

If it is true, as has been argued, that our problem with socialism resides inside each human being, then it must follow that the cure for socialism is one which must be self administered. You cannot control any other person. This is a physical impossibility. Your rights are unalienable, even by your own willingness and connivance to alienate them.

The cause of individualism and human liberty is too important a cause to be entrusted to any organization or group of men. Only YOU can improve yourself to the point where you are competent and capable of defeating socialism within yourself. Only by so doing can you become able to serve the cause of freedom for all men.

SYLLOGISMS

Socialist Syllogisms

Equation: MMW = X ÷ A (Man's Material Well-Being

equals All Land and Property

divided by the Number of

Human Beings in Existence)

ECONOMIC

1. All men are of equal value.

2. No one man is entitled to more than any other man
   has.

3. There is a limited amount of land (and other property)
   in existence.

4. Therefore, it is necessary to insist on an equal division of all property among all men.

ON THE NATURE OF MAN

1. Individually, man has neither merit nor value. It is
   only as man serves the collective that merit or value
   is discovered.

2. Since those who have more than others will not relinquish their advantages voluntarily, force must be used.

3. This force must take the form of:

   A. Marxist idea

   Violent overthrow of governments which are protecting private ownership. Replacement of these governments by democratic forms which will do the bidding of the workers and will form a "dictatorship of the proletariat."

   B. Fabian idea

   Gradual infiltration of existing governments by peaceful means, until all governments legally remove all rights of private ownership.

4. When the force of government has thus been employed, the socialist Utopia will be achieved — a state of universal division of all wealth and the creation of a society in which there are neither rich nor poor.

A. The apparent contradiction between this presumption and the socialist economic presumption is found in the explanation that whereas all men are equal in value, the value is nil until service to the collective has been demonstrated.

2. The man who serves himself and does not serve the state has no right to live.

3. All production is for "society" and no individual has a right to own anything.

4. If "society" is enriched by the services of individuals, it will follow that all of "society" will benefit by that enrichment.

5. A "society" shorn of its non-conformists is a superior society.

6. The state shall be the only capitalist.

POLITICAL

1. To have a moral world, division of property among men must be on an equal basis.

Individualist Syllogisms

Equation: MMW = NR + HE × T (Man's Material Well-
Being equals Natural
Resources plus Hu-
man Energy times
Tools)

ECONOMIC

1. Each man is an individual and no two are alike.

2. Each man is entitled to all that he can himself produce.

3. No man is entitled to something that he has not produce.

4. Man's nature is such that if he is free to make a profit or to run the necessary risks involved in seeking to make a profit, he will produce most abundantly.

5. No man can make a profit at the expense of others, for any profit that comes to him via the usage of the free market is a profit voluntarily provided by other men in a free society who have also profited by his energies.

ON THE NATURE OF MAN

1. Man has a right to live.

2. Man has a right to produce in order to live.

3. Man has a right to own that which he produces.

4. Man has a right to keep or to dispose of what he owns according to his own wisdom and conscience.

POLITICAL

1. All political action is at once collective and coercive.

2. No individualist wishes to partake of collectivist or coercive activity.

3. Therefore, no individualist will participate in political action.

I AM THE SPIRIT OF LIBERTY

With me life has purpose and meaning.

Infinite variety is mine, and Paradise beckons those

who love me and know me.

Embrace me — and the commonplace becomes high

adventure; the infinite becomes real.

Turn your back upon me, and you are doomed to

conformity and monotony.

I AM THE SPIRIT OF LIBERTY

When you look into my eyes, you must forsake all

others.

With me there is solitude and grandeur. I cannot abide

fear and the fearful, and the huddling together

of masses.

Throughout all recorded time, I have stood with the

brave.

Those who have known my smile have dared the

impossible.

I AM THE SPIRIT OF LIBERTY

If you live with me, you will achieve gloriously.

I do not promise success. But with me, even a failure is magnificent.

I disdain groups and collections of people.

I am always alone. But I am never lonely. If you aspire to my radiance you will experience the joy of creation. You will know the unalloyed thrill of accomplishment.

I AM THE SPIRIT OF LIBERTY

I am with you all the way — or I am not with you.

You must be loyal to me with all that you have and are.

Join me and we are both indivisible.

You must give your ear only to my voice.

The siren songs of security, and benefits at the expense of others are alien to me.

You must give no heed to those who promise regulations and controls, all in the name of happiness and peace.

There are other and easier paths to follow than the one you must travel if you come with me.

But if you abandon me — you and generations to come will drift into oblivion and death.

Sometimes the snow and ice of apathy and indifference cover me. Yet you must know that so long as life endures, a spark of me can be fanned into a flame.

I AM THE SPIRIT OF LIBERTY